Pilgrimage Home

The Conduct of Contemplative Practice in Groups

Gerald G. May

PAULIST PRESS
New York/Ramsey/Toronto

Library of Congress
Catalog Card Number: 78-61720

ISBN: 0-8091-2143-3

Published by Paulist Press
Editorial Office: 1865 Broadway, New York, N.Y. 10023
Business Office: 545 Island Road, Ramsey, N.J. 07446

Printed and bound in the
United States of America

Contents

Preface

This book is meant to be a resource for anyone who is engaged in helping others grow in spiritual awareness. It includes the insights, thoughts and experiences of Shalem's seven years of working with spiritual formation. Shalem (pronounced "shahlaim") is the Institute for Spiritual Formation which was formed as part of the Metropolitan Ecumenical Training Center in Washington, D.C.

The learnings in this book relate to what we feel to be some of the most important areas of spiritual formation in modern Western society. Part I, *Beginnings*, contains a brief history of Shalem and our early experiences and discoveries in the area of spiritual leadership. Part II, *Learnings*, addresses the basic understandings and insights we have accumulated through our experience, and should provide a conceptual framework from which group contemplative practice can be approached. Part III, *Practice*, gives specific suggestions for the establishment and conduct of contemplative spiritual growth groups. Part IV, *Perspectives and Critique*, presents the views of different modern spiritual leaders on the areas previously discussed, as well as questions and criticisms which have been raised regarding our work.

Many people have participated in the process of examining and distilling Shalem's experience so that the present book could come into being. A two year grant from the Lilly Endowment funded the study.

The basic study group consisted of the following people:

Gerald G. May, M.D., Psychiatrist, who coordinated the study and authored the book.

Parker Palmer, Ph.D., Dean of Studies at Pendle Hill, a Quaker-sponsored living and learning community near Philadelphia. Parker contributed great stimulation and critique, as well as the major emphasis on historical and community aspects of the study.

Jean Haldane, religious educator, researcher, and congregational consultant. Jean was helpful in developing interviewing techniques and ways of processing information during the early part of the study.

Roy Oswald, M.Div., Director, Clergy and Congregational Development, METC, who was primarily responsible for the practical refinement and application of the self-search format, conducted the first wave of interviews with Shalem participants, and contributed very helpful theological considerations to the study.

Tilden Edwards, M.Div., Executive Director, METC and Director of Shalem, who conducted the extensive interviews of modern spiritual leaders, prepared the difficult material for Chapter 12, and arranged a national conference with spiritual leaders for the purposes of clarifying and enriching the understandings which have proceeded from this study.

Administrative assistants for the study, all of whom contributed many helpful ideas and suggestions as well as practical assistance, were:

Devera Ehrenberg-Kaim
Winifred Conley
Carole Roush
Judith McCallum-Moe

Invaluable help in the form of consultation and critique came from:
James Forbes, D.Min., Associate Professor of Homiletics and Worship, Union Theological Seminary, New York.
Carole Crumley, M.Div., Interim Rector, Christ Church, Washington Parish.
Daniel Polish, Ph.D., Associate Director of Synagogue Cuncil of America, Washington, D.C.
Dolores Leckey, M.A., Executive Director, Secretariate of the Laity, National Conference, Catholic Bishops.
Henry Atkins, M.Div., Vicar, Community of the Advent, Washington Parish.
Barry Evans, M.Div., Staff, College of Preachers, Washington Cathedral.
Urban Holmes, Ph.D., Dean, St.Luke's School of Theology, Tennessee.
Vincent Cushing, STD, President, Washington Theological Union, Washington, D.C.
Sallie TeSelle, Ph.D., Dean, The Divinity School, Vanderbilt University, Nashville, Tennessee.

The Rev. William Moremen and Ms. Marlene Maier were greatly supportive and helpful in testing the Self-Search Format with their groups.

We are deeply indebted to all those Shalem participants who took the time and effort to answer our questions and make suggestions for the study.

The study itself was not research in the usual sense of the word. We did gather data and spend considerable time attempting to refine our ways of dealing with the data. We continually re-assessed our assumptions and hypotheses. But this was no cold, objective study of things *about* spiritual growth. It was rather a growing process in and of itself. Though at the beginning we thought we might be able to objectify certain aspects of our study, it soon became apparent that such objectification would cause us to lose the sense of what we were really about. So the study became a part of our own pilgrimage together, a vital process of learning at a deep and personal level.

The process of the study was difficult at times, hilarious at others, and always stimulating. We in the study group are very grateful to all those people who helped us, and we hope that the substance of this book will do justice to their efforts and their caring.

It has been fun to work on this book, primarily because of the delightful and dedicated people who have worked with me. But the work has also been enriching at a very personal level. Many areas of my own pilgrimage have been clarified and deepened in the process, and I am left with a more profound sense of humility and awe as I sense the mystery of what we are trying to do.

In putting this material together, I have tried to reflect the orientation and understandings of Shalem's leaders and participants as clearly as possible through the clouds of my own bias. And though I have written these words, the message and most of the work behind them has come from others. All of the people mentioned above contributed immeasurably to the study and to the preparation of this book. Each chapter has been read, re-read, revised and critiqued by several of Shalem's workers and the entire manuscript has been submitted to a large number of spiritual leaders and theologians for their comments. Thus this book grows out of many people, representing a variety of Western and some Eastern religious traditions.

One thing which all of these people have in common is a reverent quest to be of service to the growth of others. I assume that readers of this book will share this quest.

It is my hope, as it is the hope of the entire Shalem study group, that this book will offer some real help along this path.

Gerald G. May
Columbia, Md.
January 1978

Introduction

"Something Spiritual"

One of the most difficult aspects of discussing spiritual growth is trying to discern just what it is that one is talking about. "Spirituality" has become such a tossed-about term in recent years that it seems to have lost much of whatever specific meaning it once had. One person says, "My spiritual life is my relationships with other people." Another says, "Spirituality for me is going to church and reading the bible." Still another says, "Spirituality is coming into harmony with God, true liberation and salvation." And then someone says, "It seems to me that *all* of life is spiritual. There's nothing that isn't spiritual."

The word itself, based in "spirit" and reflecting something as basic as respiration, does surely refer to deep and vital levels of our being. It does surely raise the possibility of truth which lies beyond our usual perceptions of life. And usually, it refers to some aspiration towards the undergirding of our lives with meaning and reverence.

But we have learned repeatedly that words cannot do justice to what we are about. First, there is no way to choose words which everyone will find acceptable. Trying to be "ecumenical" by presenting a broad framework of interpretation of our terms, we will inevitably alienate people of strongly conservative orientations. Second, there simply *are* no words to describe the deepest levels of human spiritual experience. We can only hope that the essence of our search will become more clear as we tell the story of our pilgrimage.

To begin with, our pilgrimage is taking us home. Nearly all of us who

1

have participated in Shalem had strong ties with modern American religious institutions. But while many other people seemed to be able to find adequate religious fulfillment in the routine activities of their churches or synagogues, we were not satisfied. All of us felt in one way or another that there was "something" missing in our religious experience. As will be seen in the pages that follow, we have come to label that something as "spiritual."

There was perhaps some selfishness in the attitude we had. We were looking for the church to provide something for us, to meet some need within us, and we were frustrated when it did not. Perhaps in this there may be some reflection of what has been called the "me generation" or the "new narcissism," in which people seek more to meet their own needs than to ask what they can do for others. To be sure, we were aware of needs within ourselves; needs which we felt somehow should have been met, or at least more fully acknowledged by our existing religious institutions. And not finding that kind of sustenance, we began to come together and search for it "on our own." Yet most of us have remained committed and active within our churches, congregations, and communities during the time of our pilgrimage. And even more importantly, most of us have found that our searching, though it has taken us into arenas which at first seemed very alien to our traditional religious backgrounds, has brought us more fully and deeply *back* into those very traditions. This is the meaning of "Pilgrimage Home."

For us, this is the meaning of any true pilgrimage. A pilgrimage is a journey, of experience if not of geography, into new and seemingly uncharted territory, *but it is not a one-way trip*. With vision somewhat more clear as a result of the journey, one can discover a richness within one's own heritage which had previously been overlooked. A richness which had been there all along, but to which one's eyes simply had not been open.

It is this learning which constitutes the most important offering of this book; an assurance that by exploring varying approaches to spirituality, an individual is not doomed to separate himself or herself from the religious roots from which s/he has come. Rather, such exploration can deepen one's commitment to those roots and enable one's daily religious life to become much more vital and dynamic.

These roots are very important. Narcissism and self-centeredness are dangers inherent in nearly any form of spiritual practice. If these dangers are to be minimized, *it is vital that one locate oneself within the context of one's history and one's community*.

From time to time we will speak of present centeredness, of self-examination, and of solitude. But the present moment needs to be recognized as the immediate manifestation of history, the self needs to be seen as one piece of humankind, and solitude must be understood as preparation for involvement. To forget one's place in history and community is not only to ask for alienation and escape from social responsiveness, it is also to search without any sense of home base, direction, or destination.

But still the question remains. What is the destination? What is the search really for? We have tried, many times and in many ways to define it. But always when we seem close to a definition that really fits, something backfires. There's always something excluded by our definition, or the definition has killed through objectification the living essence of what we seek.

Perhaps it is that like the medieval Christian mystics, we are seeking direct awareness of God, and that this is so ineffable that words fail utterly. Yet we have all come to acknowledge in one way or another that we are not saints. We are human beings entrapped in our very human predicament, and we have to affirm that predicament. Most of us also recognize, by now at least, that if union with God in the mystical sense is to occur, it will occur on God's terms and not as a result of our "achieving" it.

Many of us might say that we wish to deepen our awareness and realization of our relationship *with* God or Christ; to be in greater harmony with Divine Will. But this too is not fully adequate, for it often seems to raise too much of a sense of separation *from* the Divine.

There are those of us who would say that what we seek is simple clarity of awareness; the capacity to perceive life as it actually is, free of our personal attachments and preconceptions. Others would say that it is peace we seek, the peace that passeth all understanding. Still others might call it enlightenment, a state just as impossible to define.

Most of us would agree that within the vast realm of human experience, there is an ultimate concern which can be called "religion," and within the realm of religion there is an arena of direct experience, of immediate feeling, of vital personal and community awareness which can be called "spirituality." Finally, within that arena of spirituality, there is a group of traditions which seek increasing harmony with and closer realization of the Divine through the means of silence and open awareness in daily life. These traditions can be called "contemplative," and it is here that our paths have taken us. But though this may be a clarification of our journey, it is still far from a definition.

Even though we can try to appreciate our grounding in history, and even though we can acknowledge the inadequacy of words in describing our goal, there is still some anxiety about not being able to define precisely what our destination is. But this is where it has been so helpful to be together, to share a sense of community in the search. For no matter how each of us may try to define the goal and no matter what words we use to describe our experience, it becomes clear in so many ways that we *are indeed searching for the same thing*. This commonality of longing, based in history and verified in community, affirms the legitimacy of our struggle. It enables us to receive *sustenance from* those around us, and, at times, to lose our self importance in *service to* those around us.

And even though we cannot precisely define what it is we seek, it is good to keep trying. Because if we don't, we may find ourselves becoming locked into subtle, even unconscious assumptions and preconceptions which can only cloud our vision and impede our course. In this regard, we shall from time to time throughout the text of this book attempt to clarify our approaches rationally. In the meantime, suffice it to say that most of our search and most of our methodology is summed up by a simple phrase which makes its appearance in many of our beginning groups as a base for quiet prayer. For us, it signifies the eternal mystery of contemplative practice.

"BE STILL, AND KNOW THAT I AM GOD."

Part I
Beginnings

1

Shalem—A Brief History

Historians of the future will probably look back upon the 1970's as a time of spiritual re-awakening in America. Contemplative spirituality has been alive since the dawn of each great world religion, but for generations in America it has been relegated to the background, limited to fringe groups or closely knit sects. It was not until the early 1970's that it assumed more popular proportions. Most of us who are connected with Shalem would identify the early seventies as the time we began to identify the existence of a fresh stage of our own spiritual quest.

I was in Pennsylvania at the time, directing a drug abuse program in a rural county. Though I didn't know him then, Tilden Edwards was in Washington D.C., working as the director of the Metropolitan Ecumenical Training Center.

Both of us were experiencing the feeling that something was missing in our professional and personal lives. In my work as a psychiatrist, I was frustrated by the realization that though I could help people with their interpersonal and intrapsychic problems, there was still a longing within them for something deeper; something for which I had no answers. And in Tilden's work as an Episcopal priest and director of METC, he was discovering that there were levels of spiritual need in the clergy and in congregations which simply were not being touched. At the time, Tilden was able to recognize that the "something missing" was "something spiritual." I still didn't have a name for it.

It wasn't until I began talking with people who had fully overcome

7

their addictions that I started to think in terms of "spiritual." These
people told me that what had enabled them to move beyond addiction
was not psychotherapy, social work or will power. Instead, they all
described an experience, amazingly common to them all, of suddenly
feeling at one with the world, peaceful and relaxed with things just-as-
they-are; an experience of fully being alive in this very moment. Some of
them described this in religious terms, calling it the direct experience of
God or of having the Holy Spirit come upon them. Others described it in
existential-philosophical terms. Still others couldn't find any words at
all. One man said simply, "I guess I just found equanimity."

Something about this experience had clicked, synthesized, and
integrated deep within these people's being. And life was simply not the
same for them afterwards. Hearing this story caused something to resonate within me, in my heart as well as in my professional curiosity. There
was more to life than trying to live. There was something which could
make living a beautiful, awesome, and incredibly *simple* process. Something which could give life grounding. Something spiritual. This is what
my patients and clients had been longing for. And I realized that I longed
for it, too.

Tilden's experience was similar. In his past he had known a little
about "religious experience," "mystical states," and the numinous quality of spiritual realization, but these had seemed distant from the daily
social, political, and interpersonal realities which had pressed in on him
so hard during the late 1960's. Now, they did not seem so distant. There
was an unfolding sense in Tilden and in some of his co-workers that
without a solid spiritual base, none of their efforts could be truly real or
basically trustworthy. Tilden began to take a hard look at the spiritual
roots of his life and work.

Tilden and I responded to our similar discoveries in similar ways.
For a while we tried to approach the problem objectively, he through an
empirical study of spiritual maturity, and I through a clinical study of the
psychodynamics of spirituality. His work resulted in a paper* in which
he found that many of the people labeled as spiritually mature by their
clergy were simply those who seemed to have the best facility in interpersonal relations. Here, too, there seemed to be something missing; it
seemed people's energies were directed outward to the exclusion of an
inner awareness of spiritual truth and centeredness in being. My work
resulted in a paper also,** which described how people found it difficult

---

*"Spiritual Growth: An Empirical Exploration of Its Meaning, Sources, and Implica-
tions," METC, Washington, D.C., 1974.
  **"The Psychodynamics of Spirituality," Journal of Pastoral Care, Vol. XXVIII No.
2, June 1974.

and threatening to speak directly about their spiritual needs and experiences.

These objective studies satisfied neither Tilden nor myself, and both of us were drawn to a more personal exploration. I learned what I could about meditation, contemplative prayer and healing, and for the first time in my life I began what could be called a personal spiritual practice.

Tilden, on sabbatical, found himself attending an intensive program led by the Tibetan Buddhist Lama Tarthang Tulku, followed by an extended Ignatian retreat.

By 1973 I had decided that whatever course my future professional work was to take, it would have to deal somehow with the relationship between psychology and spirituality. Shortly thereafter, Roy Oswald told me he was going to work with METC, and gave me a copy of Tilden's sabbatical paper.* I sent Tilden some of my work and later we arranged a meeting.

When we met, Tilden told me about some of the first steps he'd taken with contemplative group work through METC. He spoke of the paucity of "realized masters" from whom to learn, of the importance of protecting them whenever they are found, and of the necessity for most people to conduct their spiritual searching with less-than-perfect leadership. He told me of his misgivings about his own competence in beginning contemplative work with clergy and congregations, and I shared with him my own feelings of spiritual inadequacy. Yet we both agreed that so many people we knew were crying out for help with their spiritual growth that, as inexperienced as we were, we had to respond in some way.

Tilden told me he had led a couple of spiritual retreats and some congregational work, and that he had also started a long-term group with about twenty people who had committed themselves to a personal and collective search for spiritual deepening.

We met again several times after that, and then he asked me to attend a retreat with his long term group. It was very rich, that first experience with the group. I was impressed with the beauty and impact of Tibetan chants and visualizations, and amazed at how some of the physical postures and breathing exercises helped to clear my mind. But most of all I was struck by how amazingly "Christian" it all seemed. Here was this group of people, most of them Roman Catholic, Episcopal, or other Christian clergy and laity, meeting at a Roman Catholic retreat center, doing yoga and chanting Sanskrit syllables at one moment

---

*"Summer Report," METC, Washington, D.C., 1973.

and sharing eucharist the next. Morning and evening prayer in the chapel. At meals, after saying a very Protestant-sounding grace, there was a very Buddhist sort of silence in which everyone was "mindful," watching hands moving, feeling mouth chewing, sensing the meal. Then the Jesus prayer, silently, in time with breathing in the afternoon. And Sufi dancing at night.

Lots of "stuff," yet all very quiet, and all somehow very Christian. It rattled the bones of my Methodist background and left me with deep wonder. I recalled, strangely, my first communion. I had been six years old, and my parents had quietly indicated they felt I was "old enough," and that made it very special. Back in the pew afterwards, lying down with my head on my mother's lap and my feet in my father's, it was very warm. I remembered that I had thought then, "Now I am really a Christian." It had meant something to me then, when I was six, some-thing I'd long since forgotten. And now, at this retreat, I was both encouraged and somewhat frightened by the possibility that I might be starting to remember.

It wasn't until much later that I understood the importance of the basic Christianity of that retreat, and of Tilden's overall approach. I had assumed that the "something spiritual" I sought would be found some-where outside traditional Christianity. Probably in Yoga or Zen. But now it seems that the Eastern methods are not at all substitutes for the religion of my fathers. Rather, they are ways back into the heart of that religion: ways of clearing one's vision for what is there and has been there all along. Pathways home.

Later, Tilden asked me to join that long term group and to co-lead a group of my own with Dolores Leckey. Tilden thought Dolores and I would complement each other well, with my rather secular-psychological-humanistic orientation and her deep Roman Catholicism.

I felt anxious about meeting her at first, as I would about meeting anyone who was supposed to "complement" me. But we did comple-ment each other beautifully. I could not be in her presence without absorbing just a little of her reverence, and she delighted in how lightly I could take the usually heavy significance of spirituality.

About the same time, I got to know the other people who were eventually to become Shalem's primary leadership. Bill Moremen, a gentle UCC pastor, struggling to integrate the administrative and social responsibilities of a big-city church with the incredible calm of silence. Marlene Maier, an Episcopal laywoman, quiet and smiling on the out-side, but fiercely strong and curious in her faith. Cecilia Braveboy, the administrative assistant of METC, striving for an integration of her Roman Catholic and African heritages. Barry Evans, an Episcopal priest on the staff of the College of Preachers, sternly sensing the importance of liturgy, seeing silence in the flow of ritual.

There were others to come in the months and years that followed. Henry Atkins, priest, Zen student, and ardent social activist. Jim Forbes, sweet but penetrating sharer of his black and Pentecostal heritage. Dan Polish, rabbi full of humor and insight. Carole Crumley, Episcopal seminarian. Richard Byrne, Paulist Father. Emma Lou Benignus, Episcopal lay leader. These people were to form the leadership group which planned the formation and growth of Shalem.

By 1974, we had recognized the need for a more coherent institute for spiritual formation. We felt it was time to take the varied groups, retreats, conferences and consultations which METC had sponsored and coordinate them within a single program for spiritual development. In the fall of 1975, Shalem became a formal entity.

It was not without some trepidation that this step took place. We were all aware of the dangers of becoming too institutionalized. It would raise the temptation to make what we were doing "special." And it might lead us to think of spiritual growth as an object to be manipulated or a product to be sold. And there was always the possibility that the subtle truth of what we were about would be lost in the "business" of it all.

These concerns led us to seek opinions from others who had been watching our work. One of the people we asked was Tarthang Tulku Rinpoche, who had visited us several times during the previous two years and had become a kind of warm Tibetan Granddaddy to us all. When we asked him, Tilden, Barry, Dolores and I were sitting with Rinpoche at a Chinese restaurant near the Washington Cathedral where he'd just met with some of our group members. Rinpoche had with great zest just finished a monumental meal including huge quantities of hot mustard, during which the extent of his conversation had been, "mmmm-hot." Tilden sat up straight in his chair and carefully began describing our thoughts about forming an institute for spiritual development. He listed our fears and apprehensions. He ended with the big question: "Rinpoche, we'd like to know what you think. From what you know about us, do you think we're ready to begin this kind of work without distorting it too much?"

Rinpoche glanced up from some residual crumbs on his plate, smiled and said, "Of course. You have no desire to do harm, do you?"

A rather unspecial sort of blessing for our new institute. Perhaps we'd been trying so hard to keep it from being special that it had in fact become special. At any rate, Shalem began. And since then under its aegis there has been a growing number of offerings: more long-term groups; "specialty groups" for psychotherapists, prisoners and seminarians; retreats, workshops, congregational consultations; conferences and publications, and the Lilly Endowment-funded study which has resulted in this book.

In retrospect, Tilden's question to Rinpoche that day entailed more than asking for a blessing. It was a very clear expression of our concern about being seen as "spiritual leaders." Could we, in the realization of our own spiritual immaturity, really presume to be teachers, leaders, or even facilitators of others? Tilden has recently written a book* in which he describes his initial feeling about beginning this work as "the blind leading the blind." It was a feeling we all shared. Even now, even at our best, we are no more than the one-eyed person in the land of the blind.

Living Simply Through the Day. New York: Paulist Press, 1977.

2

In the Land of the Blind: Beginning Experience With Group Leadership

The individual spiritual search is a subtle and delicate process. It often seems evanescent, and it is frequently marked by extremes of lassitude and asceticism, waxing and waning of confidence, and periods of total confusion interspersed with moments of incredibly clear understanding. Thus, while spiritual truth may be utterly simple, the search for that truth often seems awesomely complex.

If the individual search can appear to be that complex and confusing, the role of spiritual leadership is even more so. Pilgrims always seem to have incredible difficulty with spiritual leaders; finding them in the first place, trusting them and following them once they are found, and separating from them when the time for leaving has come. And spiritual leaders themselves often struggle with feelings of presumptuousness, inability, and the fear that their own wills and egos will get in the way of the Ultimate.

The words of truly realized masters concerning this predicament would probably be reassuring. They would indicate that good will and a humble and open heart are all that is necessary to help another on his or her spiritual quest, and that those of us who "struggle" with the role of spiritual leadership are creating too many problems for ourselves. But it

13

seems the struggle is necessary. At least it has been for us. We have experienced the struggle from both sides; looking for spiritual leaders for our own growth, and trying to be spiritual leaders for others.

Finding Leaders

As beginning pilgrims ourselves, most of us had tended to view spiritual development as an objective to be achieved in the most efficient possible way. We had not found adequate contemplative spiritual leadership in our regular churches and congregations, so we began to look elsewhere. But at the same time, few of us were ready to commit our precious spiritual infancy to an alien tradition. At least, that is, without being assured that we would get what we wanted. And guarantees are hard to come by in legitimate spiritual traditions.

Looking back upon the heavy seriousness with which most of us consciously entered the spiritual path, we may be tempted to smile. But the confusion was real then. And we must admit that we are not at all free of it now. It may take more subtle forms, but we continue to find ourselves attached to our own spiritual growth; trying to "do" it, making it heavy and cumbersome, dramatic and tragic.

For the beginner, as well as for us "more experienced" beginners, the question remains, "What is one to do about choosing spiritual leadership?"

An extremely eclectic teacher is one option; a person who will expose one to a wide variety of approaches in the hope that a few of the pellets from his or her spiritual shotgun will strike near the heart. There are many highly eclectic programs available, and many people have found them helpful. Still, too much eclecticism leads to superficiality.

Another way, which a number of Shalem participants have followed, is to adopt a personal eclecticism which enables them to dip into a variety of traditions as they travel along their personal paths. The hope here is that though there may be eclecticism in terms of technique and discipline, there will at the same time be a deep constancy to the individual's personal search.

Still another possibility is to go ahead and commit oneself deeply to a certain tradition, casting aside worries about the other possibilities which were not chosen, and hoping that once one has "completed the course," one will be able to return home again.

There are problems with all of these approaches, not the least of which is that spiritual formation is seen as something primarily under the control and direction of the individual, leaving little room for God's own guidance. Or spiritual growth may be seen as an objective; something to be attained, in which case it again becomes the slave of the individual's autonomous will. Or one may fall into a quasi-psychological search for the satisfaction of personal needs to the exclusion of commitment to the world and to society. Those who truly feel that their spiritual growth is the work of God and not of themselves are indeed fortunate, for they need not be concerned with all this deliberation. But the trouble is that most people who feel spiritual hunger also feel they must somehow take charge of their own growth. Then they are committed to struggle with these dangers.

Early Anxieties

As Tilden, Dolores and I began our roles as leaders in Shalem's spiritual development groups, our definition of these hazards was hazy, but we were well aware that dangers existed. We were afraid of leading too much, of going too far, of pressing too hard. At the time, our fears often took on a psychological flavor. What if somebody became hysterical as a result of some meditation experience? What if we encouraged someone to go beyond the limit of their ability to cope? What if we were leading them in the wrong direction altogether? What power we gave ourselves!

The one reassuring aspect in all of this was our deep conviction that the spiritual growth of people was not ultimately up to us. The power was not ours, but utterly beyond us. Still, there were times for all of us when we were accosted by worries about whether we could handle the task well, thereby trying to see ourselves as the ones who were "doing" the spiritual growth of others. And there were times when we tried so hard that we had indeed "gotten in the way." It is not altogether pleasant to admit to this kind of egocentrism, but on the other hand it is necessary to acknowledge that most human "spiritual leaders" are bound to fall prey to it from time to time.

We have now come to see our role as that of *helping people find ways of opening* themselves to the Divine power beyond all of us. And our primary concern is to get out of the way of whatever growth or development is to take place. Though we may now be a little lighter and not so dramatic about all of this, it remains a guiding principle, and one we often fall short of.

Prayer seems absolutely necessary for this. Prayers that we will not get in the way. Prayers that our leadership will not drive people off the track of their own natural spiritual awakening. "Thy will be done" prayers. And simple prayers that what happens will be good and not bad.

I remember my own anxieties around the time of beginning leadership of a spiritual development group. It was not the kind of leadership, nor the kind of group that I had been used to. It was not a therapy group, not an encounter group, not a church service, not a conference or seminar or traditional prayer group.

My apprehension was made up of a mixture of factors. There was that overriding concern that I would get in the way. There were worries about conflicts of religious belief among the participants, and there were concerns about the psychological well-being of those involved. Mixed in with these were my own ego investments, concerns about acceptance and rejection by others, success and failure, and meeting expectations.

It was very good to have Dolores with me at that time. Her faith gave us both more confidence, but what helped us the most was the gentle openness of the participants. They understood our concerns, and were very easy with their expectations. And thankfully, they did not expect Dolores or myself to do their spiritual development for them.

In spite of all this support, and the beginning realization that people have sufficient spiritual and psychological defenses which naturally prevent their going too far too fast, I still felt I had the power to goof it all up. That of course was just another way of saying, "It's all up to me." In becoming so terribly conscious of my deficiencies, I was still holding onto my sense of personal power.

This became clear to me one day when Tilden and I were sharing some of the concerns we felt about "trying to be leaders." I told him that though I had for a long time felt very uncomfortable about praying for things, I had been finding it very helpful to pray before each group started. It was comforting to be able to "offer up" the fate of the group meeting. I said, "It helps me to feel more comfortable during the group meeting and it actually seems that the group goes better. Maybe it's just that I'm more relaxed. But somehow it does go better. But then when it's time for the next group, there I am, anxious again."

Tilden nodded, indicating that he'd had similar experiences. "Maybe," he said, "you keep getting anxious because all you do is pray for help with your anxiety. Do you ever say 'Thanks' after a group goes well?"

No, I hadn't. It was easy to give God the responsibility when I was afraid things wouldn't go well. But then, if they *did* go well, *I* would prefer to take the credit.

Tilden, Dolores, Marlene, Bill and the others who began to lead groups in subsequent years all experienced their own forms of these concerns. Each of us, in his or her own way, was and still is somewhat uncomfortable with being seen as a spiritual leader. Yet somehow each of us needs to do it.

Leadership Roles

One of the ways we have dealt with these problems is to try to be open with the groups about our own uncertainties. Not to make a big deal of them and turn it into a "please support me in my weakness" session, but simply to be honest about our experience and not pretend to be anything more or less than we are.

Another response is to see ourselves not so much as leaders of spiritual development but more as the possessors of certain "skillful means." Skillful means is a translation of the Sanskrit *upaya*, and refers to ways, modalities, techniques which are helpful in contemplative practice. In this sense, we can see ourselves as capable of teaching certain ways of moving into meditation and quiet prayer, body work, chanting, etc., which people can practice and use as needed in their spiritual journeys.

Another thing we can do is share our experience, our own spiritual journeys. In this way we can support our participants' search, affirm their struggles, and more often than not, lend a helpful perspective to their perceptions of themselves.

Finally, we can create an environment. We can establish and maintain an atmosphere which we hope will be helpful in nurturing the spiritual growth of the group's members. We do this by planning a structured rhythm and sequence for the meetings, by setting guidelines for activities and sharing within the group, and by establishing standards for the personal practice of participants on their own. In this way, we can create a sort of ritualized "nest" in which we hope the incubation of spiritual awareness will occur.

To summarize, we feel that "leaders-who-aren't-fully-developed-themselves" can contribute the following:

1. The teaching of "skillful means."
2. The sharing of personal insights and experiences.
3. The establishment and maintenance of a helpful environment.

Implicit in this way of doing things is the assumption that we can be no more than facilitators or catalysts of the growth of others. We can be participants in that growth, active and involved, but we are not "doing" it. In this regard, we have found it helpful to make a rather arbitrary distinction between "spiritual counseling" and "spiritual direction." Or, if you will, between spiritual facilitation and spiritual mastery.

Spiritual Counseling and Spiritual Direction

When we see ourselves as facilitators or counselors, it simply means that we participate intentionally in another person's spiritual growth. It is not necessary to adopt the model of master/disciple. All that is required for spiritual counseling or facilitation is that a person be sensitive to the spiritual life of others and capable of listening and responding without having to impose his or her preconceptions on the other person.

On the other hand, spiritual direction or mastery presumes that the individual will not only be open and sensitive to others, but will also direct or model a specific way of travelling the spiritual path. In this case the students or disciples actively commit themselves to the master's discipline, following his or her instruction to the utmost, struggling to reach an understanding equal to that of the master. In this case it is assumed that the master "knows," through very clear perceptiveness, exactly what is right for the student at any given time. This requires that the master be very far along the path himself or herself, and that the master's ego and self-interest are sufficiently out of the way so as to permit an unimpeded communication of truth.

This distinction is a rather arbitrary one, but it does communicate that while one may not feel at all qualified for spiritual direction, one may be capable of doing a very good job of spiritual counseling or facilitation.

To be an honest spiritual counselor or facilitator, one must continually be paying attention to one's own spiritual growth. This requires that the leader have leadership for himself or herself. The importance of this cannot be overemphasized, for it is impossible—unless one has been born into this world with a halo already in place—for a person to be sensitive and open to the spiritual growth of others if he or she does not have assistance in seeing through his or her own blind spots and preconceptions. We encourage this kind of leadership-of-leaders through expecting that group leaders be members of a group themselves, and that they be involved in a "spiritual friendship" on a one-to-one basis.

The Extent of Leadership

None of this understanding of our roles as spiritual leaders was pre-planned. Rather, it has grown out of the obvious needs and basic demands of the participants in our groups. And as it worked out, the participants have requested more of us in terms of leadership than we initially wanted to give. Most of us were prepared to be open, to listen and respond, and to do some minimal stage-setting in which the group process could take place. Most of us had had some experience in working with other kinds of "growth groups," and we were used to turning over a good deal of the responsibility to the group members. So we entered this work with an expectation that we would leave a good deal of the decision making process to the members; let them chart their own course in terms of what they wanted to do together. We were also prepared to experience and "work through" the inevitable conflicts and interpersonal dissonances involved in such decision-making processes.

But the participants would have none of this. They wanted to be directed, and at times they demanded it. They wanted to be told what to do, and they did not want to "waste time" working through power struggles or inter-personal conflicts in order to arrive at decisions. This took us somewhat by surprise, and some pains of adjustment were required.

It is important to keep in mind that these group members are very sophisticated people, and that this may have something to do with their attitude. They are in general highly educated "liberal" Christians who are used to shouldering responsibilities and making independent decisions. Many are clergy, religious, or religious educators. Most are quite familiar with group dynamics and organizational development. They all recognize the importance of independent decision-making, and for the most part they are people who would never be caught telling other people what to do. Yet here they were, demanding of us, "Tell us what to do."

A case in point is Tilden's experience with the first long-term group. In the beginning, Tilden emerged as a kind of "educated peer." He had collected some skillful means and had a sensitivity to the delicacy of people's spiritual needs. But he did not want to see himself as a spiritual authority and he didn't want others to see him that way. So his first involvements with leadership were rather tentative, and most of the time he tried to take his cues from the group as to what would be done and when, carefully checking out his own initiatives before proceeding. After the first few months he encouraged shared leadership, in which certain participants took over responsibility for some of the leading and teaching.

But by the time the group was entering its second year, the participants were resisting this delegation of leadership, and were pressing hard for a stronger hand at the helm from Tilden. Finally, during one meeting which had been scheduled to make plans for the following year's "curriculum," it was clearly expressed that the members really wanted stronger leadership. They did not want to be bothered with decision-making or with working through interpersonal power issues, and they actually felt imposed upon if they were requested to do this. They said literally, "Whatever you decide is O.K. with us, Tilden, but *you* decide."

So it was not so much out of a theoretical understanding of what people needed that leadership became more directive, but basically it was because the group would tolerate nothing less. In looking over this phenomenon, one may be reminded of the work of the Grubb Institute* which has spelled out so clearly that one of the roles of the church is to provide an opportunity for "extradependency" (dependency on another or through another to God) to balance the "intradependency" or self-reliance which characterizes so much of people's lives. Perhaps the Shalem groups have offered some of this kind of need-fulfillment for participants. Perhaps also there was a kind of wisdom emerging among the participants through which they sensed that it was a waste of time and energy to involve oneself intensively in the "working through" of interpersonal relationships and decision-making in a group which has as its primary purpose the deepening of contemplative spirituality, with its requirement of ego being out of the driver's seat. At any rate, it was out of necessity that leadership became more directive.

As groups gain more experience they seem to need less firm leadership. At the present time, beginning groups are very solidly directed and quite well planned by the leaders. Second-year groups are somewhat more flexibly directed, and that first Friday morning group, now in its sixth year, is quite open, with considerable shared leadership. It is hard at this time to draw any conclusions as to what this means. Perhaps some pressing needs for extradependent situations were satisfied and participants are now freer to resume more self-direction. More probably, the whole dimension of "who leads and who follows" is less important to the participants. They seem less attached to the problem altogether, and are more willing simply to respond to whatever needs to be done. It seems likely that as people do progress in their own spiritual growth, such issues as struggles for personal power, control over others, and submission-compliance just become less important.

While the early group members were clearly pressing for directive and authoritative leadership, certain limits were emerging as to the extent of that leadership. The participants appreciated having the structure and content of group activities planned for them. They generally wanted the curriculum to be chosen by the leadership. They wanted the leaders to set the time for silence, to direct the discussions which

---

*GRUBB INSTITUTE, EWR Center, Cloudelsey Street, London, N1 OHU, England.

followed, to be responsible for seeing that these conversations did not turn into psychotherapy or abstract theologizing. In general, they wanted the leaders to maintain an atmosphere conducive to personal and collective contemplative exploration.

In simpler words, *they wanted to be told what to do and how to do it*.

But on the other hand, *they did not want to be told what to think, feel, or believe*. There was, and is, considerable resistance against any kind of evangelizing or arbitrary interpretations of experience. While group members highly appreciate the opinions of leaders and of other group members in the interpretation of experience, those opinions must remain opinions and nothing more. There seems to be a kind of taboo against dogma. Nothing seems to "turn off" members of these groups more than someone proclaiming to know the truth. It seems very important that the truth be allowed to emerge within each individual in his or her own way.

On occasion in the early meetings of beginning groups, there are some furtive attempts on the part of group members to establish a kind of orthodoxy or consensus of belief, but these are short-lived. Presumably, these are part of the normal process of a group attempting to form some identity and of participants trying to find some identity within that group. But something about the experience of extended silence allows the approach to issues of identity and orthodoxy to become increasingly gentle and evanescent. As these issues become less important they are replaced by an emphasis on the members being in silence together and helping each other clarify their individual perceptions of the truth. "Teaching and proclaiming" are replaced by "listening and watching." In this sense the leaders' roles of skillful means, sharing and establishment of environment are simply vehicles which enable and nurture the participants' abilities to clarify and test their own understandings. This seems to be a very basic learning from our experience: namely that our offerings are *means* whereby individual growth is enhanced. The growth itself, and the ultimate interpretation of that growth, are out of our hands.

This has led us to see our work as a vehicle for pilgrimage. In this, our approach is different from those of most religious communities, which identify with a specific path to salvation or a prescribed way of being which constitutes salvation in and of itself. It is our growing sense that the proper path and the proper way of being lie in the depths of each individual's life as it is lived from day to day and year to year within the context of our society and history. We simply provide a temporary vehicle for travelling that path and for allowing it to be seen more clearly, whatever form it may take.

It would seem that this perception might be helpful to groups within congregations, seminaries or other religious institutions, groups which form for the purpose of mutual support in the exploration of contemplative spirituality. To see the group as a vehicle or an experience along the way rather than something which will be an end in itself is a very freeing perception. It eases the rough and rigid expectations with which many people come to contemplative practice, and it encourages people to be more attentive to the spiritual significance of their *entire* lives, including their working, eating, playing, responding to society, and relating with others. In this way, contemplative spirituality is not seen as an esoteric practice which leads one away from the urgent and colorful drama of living-in-the-world, but rather as an integral part and underlying principle *of* that living-in-the-world. In summary, it appears that what modern contemplative leadership can do is provide a temporary arena for deeper spiritual searching for certain people who cannot find this in their usual surroundings. But this needs to be done *within the context* of those surroundings.

It is interesting and somewhat reassuring that these perceptions, which we came to through so much trial and error, are shared by many of the contemporary leaders whom we were privileged to interview in preparation of this book. Virtually all of these women and men, who have been recognized as spiritual authorities within their own traditions, affirm that their role in helping others lies not in encouraging escape from the realities of daily life, but rather in nurturing an awareness and perceptiveness which will allow individuals to move ever more deeply and constructively *into* daily life.

In addition, they all seem to agree that they are not "doing" anyone's spiritual growth—that true guidance and growth come from beyond them. They all affirm that people must be met "Where they are," with responses geared to "what they need" rather than being forced into conformity with the leader's own agenda. At the same time, the leaders try to share their "skillful means" and their personhood as honestly and openly as they can. And reassuringly, most all seem uncomfortable with the title of "spiritual leader."

More will be said concerning our interviews with these leaders in Chapter 12, but at present a few quotes will help to communicate the commonality of their perceptions of leadership:

Mark Dyer, Missioner for Clergy Spiritual Formation, Episcopal Diocese of Massachusetts:

"We can set the environment, but gift is what comes; all you can do is be faithful."

Father Stephen of Our Lady of the Holy Cross Monastery:

"I do nothing; just listen."

Korean Zen Master Seung Sahn Soen-Sa:

"Good teachers are blue mountains, blue skies . . . I cannot help anyone. I point the direction; it's your job to do it."

Spiritual leadership, whether it be of the masterful kind or of the facilitative kind, seems to amount to something very simple. A pointing of direction, a setting of environment, a sharing of oneself, and a deep attentiveness. The actual understanding and growth must come as they come, through each of us. We may have the help of God, of group, of community, of friends and of "leaders" in this, but ultimately it happens individually; alone. The spiritual search is often a very lonely enterprise, even in the midst of all the support and love around us. All of us in Shalem have felt this, and we have come to see the intricacies of solitude and community as being worthy of very careful attention.

Part II

Learnings

3

"Alone and Together"

The Role of Relationship in Contemplative Practice

In gathering data for this book, one of the questions we asked our participants was how they saw their spiritual journeys as happening. The most typical kind of response is exemplified by the following: "Whatever this journey of mine really is, it happens in a solitary way. I often feel very lonely with it, and I know that in the last analysis, it is an isolated thing, very much alone. But it's funny, because I also know that without other people it wouldn't happen at all. I have so many people with me, and they're absolutely essential, but still I am alone." This combination of aloneness and togetherness appears again and again in contemplative practice. Simply stated, the paradox is that one is always and irrevocably alone in one's spiritual growth, yet at the same time one is always in the company of fellow pilgrims as well as in the company of the Divine. In true spiritual union, which is the goal for many people involved in contemplative practice, the sense of separate self is lost so that neither aloneness nor togetherness has meaning. But as long as one is on the path towards that goal there is a sense of separate self, and one must struggle with being alone or being in relationship.

There are some aspects of spiritual growth which require totally private self-confrontation, and there are other aspects which are simply so numinous that they cannot be communicated. Both of these factors make aloneness a very real and legitimate dimension of the spiritual search. Yet at the same time, there is real help available from other human beings. The support of others, their critique, guidance, and their historical heritage are not only always available in one form or another, but they are absolutely necessary.

When we look at the panorama of human spiritual searching, three basic dimensions of aloneness and togetherness seem to emerge: the solitary journey, the dyadic, and the community. In most people's lives these three overlap and intermingle constantly, but it may be helpful to look at them separately.

The Solitary Journey

There is a thread of solitude in the history of all acknowledged spiritual traditions. Perhaps it is more visible in those traditions called "contemplative," but even in approaches which are geared almost totally to group consciousness, there are still important times when each individual must turn attention inwards in order to reappraise his or her relationship to that group. And this must finally be done alone. Whether these times of solitude are formal, as in retreats to mountain caves and deserts, or whether they take place simply within one's own thoughts on a crowded street, they are times when one encounters oneself, directly and immediately. Most often these are times when social and interpersonal demands are minimized, when attention is more free to sense and experience the immediate fact of being. They are times when things settle down, when the mind clears a bit so that deeper perspectives can be gained and more basic priorities can surface. Solitude is also a time for the direct experience of spiritual reality, for becoming aware of awareness, for immediate confrontation of one's images of self. In solitude, one is thrust back upon oneself relentlessly, and one's attachments and images become devastatingly clear.

In our experience solitary prayer and meditation have been an *absolutely indispensable* component of spiritual exploration. But solitary prayer and meditation are *not at all sufficient in and of themselves*. Many of us began with an assumption that prayer and meditation are kinds of "techniques" which one applies to oneself in order to achieve greater happiness, fulfillment or realization of closeness to God. For some of us, this led to a transient period of belief that all we had to do was "Learn how to do it correctly, and do it enough," and all our spiritual longing would somehow be satisfied.

This is not an unusual way of viewing things. The popularization of recent research into the "effects" and "benefits" of meditation has greatly encouraged this kind of attitude in American society. When it was found that meditation did indeed seem to help people develop greater abilities to cope with stressful situations, psychotherapists all over the country became interested in how to "apply" various forms of meditation to their clients. And people themselves began to "apply" meditation to themselves in their search for greater happiness. This is but one example of a very prevalent attitude which tends to separate off one aspect of spiritual practice and use it as an isolated technique to achieve a secularized end.

As with thousands of other Americans, our experience with this kind of attitude has been continually disappointing. The hoped-for satisfaction never really comes, and one becomes concerned about "doing it better" or finding "a better way," and fatigue sets in. The "use" of meditation or prayer in this way will probably always prove frustrating, because it inevitably makes the contemplative technique a servant of private desire, and these private desires are always of questionable validity.

For example, one may wish to learn a certain meditation technique in order to relax. The implicit assumption here is that relaxation is good—that it will in the long run help one achieve a better life. But how can one know this for sure? We know that tension is at times a very necessary part of life. How is one to judge whether the tension one feels at any given time is basically good or bad? Such decisions are commonly made in terms of a desire—a desire which says in effect, "What is good is defined by what I want. What is bad is defined by what I don't want." The problem with this is that there is very little constancy to desire, and often very little relationship to the realities of any given situation. If there is a "purpose" to prayer and meditation, it may well be very different from the satisfactions of desire. It may well be that the "purpose" is to *move behind the vicissitudes of desire altogether*, so that "good" and "bad" are seen in a totally different light.

In addition, the use of contemplative techniques of solitude for the achievement of specific goals belies the assumption that one is enough in charge and control of one's destiny to know what it is one really needs and how to get it. This assumption is both dangerous and ironic. It is dangerous because it leads into ever-increasing spirals of attempts to conquer one's life through the personal acquisition of power forgetting the reality of God. It is ironic because most people seek out spiritual growth and contemplative methods precisely because they *don't* feel sufficiently in charge or control of their destiny.

Still, it is very common in our beginning groups to hear people using desire-based judgments such as, "I didn't have a good meditation. I just couldn't relax," or, "There was too much going on in my mind . . . I couldn't settle down." Each of us, no matter how much experience s/he has had with contemplative practice, still becomes trapped from time to time by concerns which belie our assumption that we know what "good" meditation is, and that we know what we're after, and that we know whether we're getting it or not. It is important to realize that such concerns are common, especially in contemplative solitude, and that they are probably necessary to go through. But at the same time it is important not to become seduced any more than necessary into the struggles they represent. The role of solitary prayer or meditation seems to be to get behind or beneath these kinds of issues; to encourage a depth and clarity of awareness which is not so subject to private desires and preconceptions, and to remember rather than forget that God is calling us. At this point, specific meditations are not defined as good or bad on the basis of the turmoil, drama , silence or beauty which they seem to contain. Here spiritual growth is finally seen as an inclusive process, deeply integrated with life, and not something one "does to" oneself.

In part, this is why the solitary journey is insufficient by itself. The experiences and effects of prayer and meditation need to occur in the context of daily human life, with daily human demands and responsibilities in this historical world of other human beings who are all struggling and needing, judging and preconceiving. Solitude is necessary so that the attachments, the heaviness, and the complexities of a hectic life can be burned in the fire of simple attentiveness. And community is necessary so that private desires, expectations and willfulness can be burned in the fire of corporate scrutiny and historical judgment.

People begin their formal spiritual searches with differing needs for solitary silence. Some people will find sitting still very agitating, while others will find it such a relief that they wish to do nothing else. Some people are so involved with their fellow human beings they long for solitude. Others are so lonely they find solitude deeply frightening. Therefore a program for contemplative practice needs to be flexible in terms of how hard it expects people to push themselves in solitary silence. Similarly, a program which people attend only once a week cannot press as hard in this area as might a program which people attend full-time. For example, people might attend a Zen "sesshin" and sit in meditation for many hours because there are no other demands upon them during that time. But for daily at-home practice, such long meditations are generally neither possible nor advisable. The transition between solitude and active involvement in the world comes too often and too harshly.

It is important to help each individual find his or her own most appropriate tempo for solitude. This will vary a great deal from one person to another, and for each person it will vary from one time to another. Usually it will be a kind of balance or middle path between severe austerity on one extreme and total lassitude on the other. If asked to examine their needs carefully, and if given time and support in doing this, most people will come to an understanding of this balance as it applies to them at any given time. It is helpful to have people share their experiences and struggles with solitary meditation in the group setting, for as with so many other aspects of spiritual growth, the responses of others will help immeasurably in clarifying the situation.

This flexible-yet-scrupulous kind of approach is probably much more helpful than a hard and fast prescription as to how one should spend one's solitary time. There is less chance for the harshness of bouncing to one extreme or the other. Still, it may be necessary for people to touch both extremes from time to time. Certainly most of us in Shalem have. Again in this, we had to learn from experience what the spiritual masters have tried to teach. We struggled to impose austerity upon ourselves, and our minds and bodies rebelled. We became tired and frustrated. Then we gave up to lassitude (perhaps in the hope that God would do our discipline for us), and we became lethargic. And so again through trial and error we became sensitive to a middle way. Then, Buddha's middle path and St. Francis de Sales' cautions about extremes in spiritual discipline began to make sense.

There are those who would say that the backbone of their spiritual practice has been solitary time in prayer or meditation. And for most people, this is indeed what seems to be the central focus of spiritual practice. But without other people, solitude would have neither perspective nor purpose.

The Dyadic

Just as solitude is part of every contemplative spiritual tradition, so is a one-to-one relationship with another human being. In ancient times, the spiritual dyadic was usually portrayed as a relationship of master to disciple. In modern times, it often takes the form of spiritual director and "directee," priest and parishioner, or perhaps on occasion even psychotherapist and client.

In one way or another, there always seems to be a need for some kind of guru. For many people, the role of guru has been filled by various spiritual masters, or their writings and teachings, often without the individual actually coming into physical contact with the master. Christ as a personal presence fills this role for many Christians, being seen as a living being within them. Others have found their guru in the Scriptures or the writings of Eastern and Western saints. Still others have found the guru in the person of a living spiritual teacher whom they may visit from time to time, or sometimes never even meet except through writing.

Recognizing this need for spiritual discipleship, Shalem has tried to make acknowledged spiritual masters available to participants from time to time, whenever possible. Having no hard and fast criteria as to what actually constitutes a spiritual master, we have relied on the personal experiences of some of our participants with these people. In addition, when masters come to be with our groups or lead a retreat, they are not presented with any special testimonials. Rather, they are offered like anything else, as experiences along the way. Again, what the participants may make of them is their own business. In reviewing the experience of our participants, many selected the visits by one or more of these masters as important "high points" of their time in Shalem. Besides bringing fresh insights and deep wisdom to our gatherings, these masters have provided a much-needed critique of our work and our assumptions. Perhaps even more importantly, their very presence is demonstration that contemplative practice is worth all the struggle and difficulty it entails. Our indebtedness to them will never be repaid.

While it is extremely helpful to experience such beings in the flesh, it may not be possible for small groups here and there to accomplish this. We can then be thankful that the writings of many masters are readily available, as are the personal accounts of people who have studied with them. And most of the masters themselves would say that the true guru is not necessarily in the body of a certain person. Rather, the guru exists in all things which can teach, and this means in all the experiences of one's life.

But there is more than teaching involved in a one-to-one spiritual relationship. While our participants do not wish to be told what to think, feel, or believe, they do want help in clarifying these things. Often such thoughts, feelings and beliefs are too subtle and too personal to be discussed in a group setting. So there is a need for a one-to-one relationship even if it is not that of master and disciple. Shalem has found a helpful response to this need in the concept of "spiritual friends."

At the beginning of a typical long term spiritual development group in Shalem, the participants are paired into sets of spiritual friends. Group time is set aside (usually at one group meeting each month) for these spiritual friends to meet, and some simple suggestions are made concerning the form the relationship may take.

It is understood from the outset that no matter how carefully these pairs are selected, some will "click" and some won't. We experimented with a variety of ways of selecting the pairs. We tried self-selection, asking the members to team up with someone they'd like to work with. But that raised too many interpersonal issues and seemed too "encounter-groupy" for most people's taste. On another occasion we asked people to write down what they felt they wanted and didn't want in a spiritual friend, and then the leaders tried to make the pairings based on this information. This way tended to over-objectify the people and the relationships, and it also greatly increased the participants' expectations for the spiritual friendship. It seemed to make too big a deal of it. We also tried having the group leaders do the matching based on their perceptions as to who might get along well together and who might not. This way served only to remind us of how untrustworthy our perceptions in such matters are. Often the people we thought would get along well encountered great difficulties.

After all this experimentation, we have found random pairing to be as effective as any other way, at least for beginning groups. As we have had to learn repeatedly, the simplest way is usually the best. Before the first group meets, most leaders simply pair the names of the participants at random. The only additional intervention we make is to try to pair men with women as much as possible. The reasons for this will be discussed in Chapter 7 at some length, but at present suffice it to say that we have found male-female pairs, in their complementarity, to result in greatly increased creativity and depth. On some occasions, because of an odd number of participants in the group, we have established triads as well as pairs. These generally work out well too, and have the additional advantage of helping insure a relationship if one member happens to be absent at the time of meeting.

In introducing participants to the process of spiritual friendship, we try to keep expectations to a minimum. If the friendship is presented as something very special, with potential for great depths of spiritual understanding (which indeed it has), the expectations of the members can go overboard. This creates undue self-consciousness as well as greater disappointment if the relationship does not work out well. The pairs usually meet to discuss each person's experiences and practice, but the specific style and content of their discussions are up to them.

Our suggestions to the pairs are simple. They are asked to keep each other in their prayers daily and to work out their own arrangements for meeting with each other outside the group, if they want. And we usually reserve a half-hour at the end of one group meeting per month for the pairs to get together. Some group leaders suggest that the friend given them be received as a "gift" to cultivate openness with each other. The rest is up to them.

Results of this practice have been extremely helpful to many participants, and for some, the spiritual friendship has been the most significant factor of their entire experience with Shalem. They discover the deep value of knowing that another person is keeping them in their prayers and wishing them well. They discover how helpful it is to have someone with whom to share the delicate intricacies of personal spiritual experience. And they experience a level of accountability in their personal practice that could not otherwise be achieved. For example, in the simple agreement that each person will pray for the other, or keep the other in his or her thoughts each day as part of meditation practice, there is a much greater likelihood that that daily meditation will happen. Without such a commitment, it is very easy for the demands of daily life to usurp the time of meditation. The spiritual friendship then serves as a gentle reminder to take the time. It also helps remedy the temptation to focus narcissistically on oneself. The friend is a concrete person to care for, and symbolizes everyone and everything else that also calls for our care in the world.

As is to be expected, some of the pairings will not hit it off well at all. Sometimes there are conflicts between world views, stages in life, or personalities which are so extreme they simply cannot be overcome. Other people simply may not desire a one-to-one relationship of this kind. Others already have someone outside the group who is a spiritual friend. In such situations the pair will meet only sporadically and superficially, or they may agree not to meet at all. It is important that all involved feel free to allow their spiritual friendships to evolve naturally, openly, with a minimum of willful manipulation. And they should not be made to feel guilty or inadequate if their specific friendship does not produce the dramatic fulfillment that others might.

The Long-Term Spiritual Development Group

Although it is only a temporary vehicle, Shalem's long-term spiritual development group comes closest of our offerings to approximating certain aspects of spiritual community. From the monastic orders of Christianity to the Sanghas of Buddhism, the spiritual community has always played an integral role in spiritual formation. The institutional church itself has fulfilled this role for many people. Others find their sense of community in recognizing the fact that they belong to the family of humankind, the "Body of Christ," or simply, "the people." And of course there have always been formal orders centered around contemplative spirituality. Community offers support for the basic process of spiritual searching. It validates the struggle and affirms the trials and joys and crazinesses encountered along the way. It encourages personal discipline and practice, and provides a sense of groundedness in tradition. Finally, community provides a feeling of belonging which assists people in dealing with the sensations of loneliness and isolation which inevitably accompany spiritual growth.

There are dangers in identification with community, just as there are dangers with every other aspect of spiritual growth. Perhaps the most subtle and treacherous danger is the idolatry of substituting belonging to the group for union with the Ultimate. Similarly, it is not unusual for one to substitute identification with the group for one's own diminishing self-importance. It is our impression that diminishing self-importance is an inevitable concommitant of spiritual growth, and this can create considerable anxiety within the individual from time to time. To have forgotten oneself for a while, to have ceased for a time to define oneself, can be a very threatening experience. The vicissitudes of these fears will be discussed at greater length in Chapter 5, but at present it is important to note that often people may use the identity of the group as a substitute for their own. When this happens, the individual simply transfers one kind of self-importance to another, and spiritual growth may become blocked or distorted.

This is often how groups turn into cults and sects. When enough of a group's members begin to cling to the group's identity, the group may become preoccupied with trying to define itself. It becomes caught up in delineating issues of orthodoxy and heresy and establishing group norms which its members are expected to adhere to. Then it may begin to draw circles of definition around itself, describing how it is special, and seeing differences between its members and other people. There is a certain inevitability and limited value up to this point. But any spiritual value is destroyed when, finally, the group becomes more interested in self-preservation and validation than in the growth of its members or the service they can provide. It is critical that both the membership and leadership of any group be watchful for signs of this happening.

In a spiritual development group, a member's attention is usually centered on his or her own personal needs and the quest for their fulfillment. In the beginning this is probably a quite selfish undertaking, but it can be hoped that as spiritual awareness deepens, self-centeredness will naturally expand into more open compassion for all beings. Still, this self-centered attention makes the possibility of cult-formation more likely and more dangerous. It can happen subtly, in the guise of mutual support and encouragement. Thus it becomes very important that the leaders of such groups be watchful for tendencies on the part of the membership to consolidate beliefs and assumptions, or to define themselves as special in any way. When such developments occur, they should be questioned immediately and critically. Perhaps people of very differing perspectives should be asked to join the group from time to time to provide some critical feedback.

This kind of open questioning and critique does not have to become ponderous, but we feel it should not be overlooked. It is perhaps best to maintain a light, even humorous attitude towards these dangers, not trying to insure against them by heavy defensiveness, but always alert and ready to recognize them when they may occur. Usually it suffices for the leader to ask what is behind any thought or statement which smacks of self-importance or self-definition by the group. This can help the group discern the differences between narcissism, defensiveness and true calling. It is important for the leadership to assume responsibility for this vigilance and questioning, for it is the leader who most readily can sense the tenor and direction of the group. And if the leader is being watchful for these dangers, the group itself can spend its time doing what it was meant to do, namely facilitating the deepening of spiritual awareness for the individuals involved. Such an attitude also has prevented Shalem groups from "competing" with congregational and denominational community commitments. The group is viewed as part of a larger pilgrimage together, wherein traditional denominational commitments are seen as important avenues for receiving and nurturing the full complexity and responsibility of a given heritage. Spiritual development groups are one depth point in this whole picture which can serve the renewal of those heritages, and should not be seen as substitutes or alternative communities.

In spite of these potential difficulties, the backbone of Shalem has always been the long term spiritual development group. Shalem's other offerings, such as retreats and conferences and consultations, seem simply sidelights in comparison. It is only within the long term group that people form a longer-lasting commitment to themselves and each other, thereby exposing themselves to an environment which can facilitate their contemplative practice as well as help them explore some aspects of spiritual community.

We have experimented with different sizes of groups, and have settled on a maximum membership of about twenty as the best. A smaller group would probably become more intimate and trusting on an interpersonal basis, but we have come to feel that such interpersonal emotional trusting is not as important in a spiritual development group as in other kinds of groups, and may in fact become a distraction. In a contemplative spiritual development group, the trust issue lies more in finding confidence in God than in trusting other people. There are innumerable opportunities to build trusting relationships with other human beings within secular settings, but trust in being and trust in truth is not so readily come by.

Intimacy

In this regard, a very unusual kind of interpersonal intimacy takes place in these groups; something many participants have never before encountered. By the end of a typical seven-month group, it is not unusual to find a member saying, "You know, I don't even know the last name of many of the people in my group. I have very little knowledge of their personal lives. And yet in a way I feel closer to them than I ever have to any other group of people." In fact, it is not terribly uncommon for people to emerge from seven months of weekly group meetings and not even know the *first* names of some of the members.

This kind of intimacy-in-the-face-of-anonymity may be familiar to those who have participated in prayer or meditation groups where a large part of the time is spent sitting in silence, but it seldom occurs in any other setting. In most settings, there seems to be a heavy priority placed on "getting to know each other," which results in considerable amounts of noisy social conversation or, in the case of human growth groups, emotional sharing and mutual ego need-meeting. This interpersonal noise does result in the transmission of considerable information *about* the people involved, but it often drowns out the deep reality of their being. On the other hand, to experience other people in silence is to become richly cognizant of their existence.

This is not to hold one way up over the other in terms of general interpersonal relationships, but to suggest that in a contemplative spiritual development group, the priority needs to be on silence. The fact must be faced that a group which is meeting for two or three hours once a week for several months has certain limitations of time and energy. Whatever time and energy go into establishing usual social relationships simply are not available for contemplative practice.

Most of the participants in our groups would agree that the numinous kind of intimacy which arises out of being in silence with others is a very important if not absolutely essential aspect of their spiritual growth process. Some people refer to this intimate feeling as "energy," a mystical force which is experienced whenever people go into silence together. Others speak of a sense of light. Still others describe a deep, clear sense of love which transcends the interpersonal give-and-take with which they are so familiar in their daily lives. However it is described, there is no question that the mystical qualities of silent group experience parallel those encountered in solitude, and enrich the solitary experience immeasurably.

Excitement

As is the case with solitary silence, sometimes the experience of group silence can become so dramatic and enticing that it constitutes a distraction in and of itself. It is not unheard of for prayer and meditation groups to "lock off" at the point of experiencing certain mystical phenomena, lose sight of their primary purpose of deepening the members' spiritual awareness, and proceed to try only to generate more exciting, longer-lasting and powerful mystical experiences. Again, leadership is important in helping to maintain a gently questioning perspective here, asking participants to examine not only the quality of such experiences, but where they seem to be coming from and what their value seems to be. Virtually all of our groups have encountered several occasions where during the silence one or more people experienced the same sensations, or one person seemed to influence another through his or her thoughts, or picked up a sense of what another person was struggling with. When these experiences are shared in the discussion after the silence, there is often a kind of excitement generated which, if not questioned, will encourage members to "try to make it happen again." If this goes unexamined, a good deal of time and energy can be frittered away in trying to make something exciting happen, and the end result will not only be frustrating, but will probably consist of the group having again made silence into a technique for achieving personal desires.

This problem is identical to that of dramatic visions and psychic experiences encountered in solitary silence. Such events can be so exciting and enticing that people spend months, years, sometimes even lifetimes, in "trying to make it happen." As discussed in Chapter 5 these events are probably the result of threatened self-image attempting to reassert its power and identity. But whatever their source, we are quite convinced that becoming attached to such exciting experiences constitutes a real stumbling block to spiritual growth. We would say that this includes not only dramatically beautiful or terrifying internal visions and psychic phenomena such as telepathy and precognition, but also even the gifts of healing, prophecy and speaking in tongues. Acceptance of a gift is one thing. Attachment to, or preoccupation with it is quite another.

Besides sidetracking and preoccupying the attention of group members, preoccupation with these experiences can breed a kind of competitiveness between members which can be very stifling and destructive. In sharing after the silence, it is natural for people to express meditative experiences which seemed dramatic, powerful or mystical. Sometimes the telling of such experiences becomes so colorful and dramatic that people begin to get the idea that if their meditation was not filled with exciting visions or utterly blissful silence, it wasn't quite up to par. From time to time we have heard people say, "Well, my experience in the silence wasn't as good as yours . . . nothing really happened." When this kind of value is placed on dramatic experience, the entire atmosphere of the group becomes less open, less receptive, and can at times become stifling. There is no need for this to happen, and again it is primarily the leader's responsibility to see that it doesn't. When mystical, colorful or parapsychic phenomena occur in meditation, everyone's attention will be drawn to them, including the leader's. But the leader's attention must also include what effect such events are having on the group.

It is possible to appreciate and be thankful for these events when they occur without clinging to them in any way. We see them as gifts at best, impediments at worst, but never as ends to be sought after or achieved. The best kind of attitude towards such experiences is to encourage movement *through* them, without either encouraging or deprecating them. This can happen if the experiences are acknowledged as they happen, and some gentle questions are asked about one's reaction to them, where they seem to be coming from, what effect they seemed to have on one's awareness, and how they seem to fit in the perspective of one's spiritual growth.

Silence

Shalem's spiritual development groups usually wind up demonstrating some of the factors commonly described in group dynamics, such as the tendency to try to develop a group identity, to establish a sort of hierarchy of group members, and to struggle from time to time with issues of control and competition. But in our experience none of these phenomena ever seems to preoccupy the groups, nor do they seem to last for long when they occur. When they happen, they are generally of a momentary nature, almost evanescent in their form. Silence has a great deal to do with this. The massive equalization and relaxation which occur in silence seems to dilute and detoxify many such interpersonal issues. Somehow in silence most personal and interpersonal desires, fears and struggles simply simmer down and become less important. For this reason, it is usually helpful to *begin* each group meeting with silence rather than with discussion. Discussion is necessary and helpful, but it is much more direct, simple and to the point if it follows the silence rather than precedes it.

There have been times in our groups when discussion or didactic presentations have begun to usurp the time set aside for silence in the meetings. Such situations have always been met with a demand from the group to reinstate the priority of silence. As the groups progress from year to year, silence becomes even more important and discussion less so. The times of silence become longer, and the press to achieve some special kind of experience during the silence diminishes greatly. In all groups of this kind, there is a balance which must be struck between the amount of "*space*" (silence and contemplation) and "*stuff*" (talk, activity or presentation of theory). Each group will have its own specific needs in this dimension, but in general beginning groups seem to require more "stuff." Then, as the members gain more experience with contemplative practice, there is an increasing need for "space."

Most of our participants would agree that whatever else the groups have offered, their most important contribution has been the simple opportunity for people to sit quietly together. This is clearly the aspect of group experience which members would be least willing to sacrifice. Many people have said, "I don't care what we do or what we talk about in the meetings as long as we have time to be in silence together." Many other people refer to the spiritual development groups as, "my prayer group," or "my meditation group." Still others describe "spiritual" groups they'd been in before "where all we did was talk and read *about* prayer and meditation. Now that we have an opportunity to *do* it, all the talk seems almost meaningless."

Commitment

Each of Shalem's long-term spiritual development groups consists of a number of people who have committed themselves to participation over a period of five to seven months. We would see this as a minimum duration of time required, at least for beginning groups. It takes at least this long for people to experience enough of a variety of contemplative approaches so that they can find one or more which "work" well for them. It also takes this long to begin making some inroads into the desire-laden (ego) expectations which so often tend to interfere with contemplative practice. And it takes this long to begin some integration of meditative experience with ongoing life.

Most groups begin in the fall and end in the spring, with more loosely structured opportunities to continue meeting through the summer. Then, in the following year, a more "advanced" group is offered, with less "stuff" and more "space," and an opportunity to explore a relatively few contemplative approaches in much greater depth.

A typical group meets weekly for about two hours, perhaps with a longer session once a month. Usually there are some more intensive experiences scheduled in addition to the weekly meetings, such as weekend retreats and day-long sessions. Compared with usual norms of group participation in this country, this constitutes a rather significant commitment of time and energy on the part of the participants. In fact, it seems that the degree of this commitment lies somewhere between what most people would give to a growth group and what most people would give to their church or religious community.

The quality of the commitment is also different from that entailed in both growth groups and churches. For one thing, there is a minimum of "pledging allegiance" to the group or its goals. And there is not the external sense of responsibility to the group that is encountered elsewhere, especially in religious groups. The commitment is more one that is made to oneself, out of a sense of realizing a need that must be fulfilled or a path which must be followed rather than a commitment to following standards or norms set up by a preexisting institution.

In keeping with this, there is a kind of open assumption on the part of most Shalem participants that if they find themselves travelling a different path, if they sense at any time that they need something different from what is being offered in the Shalem program, there is no obligation to continue. There is even a freedom to come in and out of the group as one's own consciousness dictates. Even though the leadership of Shalem has often attempted to place some greater structure than this on the commitment of the participants, in most cases there remains a clear, unalterable feeling that one is there because one has freely chosen to be, and that one can just as freely choose otherwise without fear of recrimination.

Almost invariably when a person leaves a long-term group, he or she announces the plans in advance, and is met with an attitude on the part of the rest of the group which in effect says, "We'll be sorry to see

you go, but we support your decision and our prayers will be with you."
Many people have indicated that one of the important things in their
group experience has been this feeling of freedom and openness about
participation. Even within each group meeting, this freedom exists. If
people are silent, no attempt is made to "bring them out" or involve
them beyond what they themselves sense is right. At least in groups
which have been meeting for more than a year or two, there seems to be
an assumption that whether a certain person speaks or is silent, or
whether another person even attends or not, the truth is the truth, and
will not be substantially influenced by the vicissitudes of human desires.
There is thus a kind of value-standard which emerges, perhaps again out
of the repeated experience of silence, in which each person must respond in the best way s/he can, based on his or her own perception of the
truth. This is very different from saying, "Whatever you desire is all
right by me," or, "If it feels good, do it." It is rather an assumption that
one's actions will be as much in consonance with one's perceptions of
truth as is possible, and further that one's actions will hopefully be
springing from that truth as it is perceived and experienced in silence.

The discernment between openness and respect for individual perception on the one hand and blind need-satisfaction on the other is not
easy. Most often this issue is clarified through the repeated process of
sharing experiences of silence and questioning, directly and forthrightly,
what they seem to mean and where they seem to be coming from. None
of us presumes to *know* the truth, but most of us presume to be developing increasing abilities to experience that truth more clearly and to allow
more and more of our action to spring from it. Such a process of
clarifying perception and operating from a dimension beneath or beyond
personal ego-desires can effectively take place only within a setting
which is open to and respectful of individual differences, and which is
relatively free of totally external demands and obligations. This is a very
important assumption, and one which will be examined in greater
theological depth later. It seems, on the surface, to run counter to much
of religious tradition which places great emphasis on people doing what
is expected of them by the church, by other people, and by God. And it
runs dangerously close at times to a free-wheeling, structureless and
narcissistic approach to life. Such are the dangers of contemplative and
mystical paths, and they must be carefully and continually watched. But
it is our feeling that if one is to grow through any intentional spiritual
"work" on oneself, then one must face up to this dilemma and walk the
line between narcissism and attachment to duty. One cannot effectively
flee to one extreme or the other here, but must continually risk the
middle-ground until such time as behavior and understanding can be

seen as springing from a dimension beyond *both* narcissism and duty.

Another, similarly delicate comment about the groups has been, "It just feels very good to be able to come and meet with a bunch of other people and not have to *do* anything." People frequently make this remark, expressing how they seem to have no other opportunities in their schedule where this kind of "just being" can happen. A question should be raised here. "Are we not simply providing little mini-vacations for people . . . times once a week when they can escape from the pressures of their daily lives? Are we perhaps not just offering escape from reality?"

To be sure, many group members do comment on how important the group is becoming to them in the context of their week, and how different it does seem from the rest of their daily activities. They may describe it as a kind of island of peace in the midst of their hectic schedules. It is entirely possible that at times the group will be used as an escape, just as solitary meditation and prayer can be used in this way. It is probably a normal and even necessary experience to go through some of this escapism, but it is also important to avoid overdoing it if possible. In this regard, it is helpful for the leader to encourage a direct and candid exploration of just what does seem to be the difference between group or individual times of silence and the rest of life. What is the difference in the quality of consciousness between the two? Who (inside us) notices the difference, and what brings it to mind? These kinds of questions, which are purely exploratory and not judgmental, can help clarify whether or not what's happening is escapism. Eventually, through this process, one might hope to see a diminishing of the sense of difference between silence and activity. But the question must still be asked as to whether the major attraction of spiritual development groups similar to Shalem's does not simply provide a momentary escape from hectic and demanding schedules. Is there perhaps nothing else, nothing more basic or constructive going on?

If such a group does constitute only an escape, it is difficult to understand why group members are so willing to stretch themselves to the very limits of endurance in some of the exercises and activities provided. Why do they struggle so hard to build an often very demanding discipline of spiritual practice on their own? And why do beginning group members place such a self-demanding premium on "doing a good job" of meditation? It may be that escape plays a role in the attraction of people to these groups, but that cannot be the only explanation. To this must be added that people feel they can willfully play a role, through contemplative practice and exploration, in their own spiritual development. Or at least in the *realization* of that development.

People generally do not sit still for long periods of time, enduring numbness and pain and itching in their bodies and constant noise in their minds if they do not feel they have at least a chance of getting something valuable out of it. Similarly, they will not fast or undergo rigorous physical exercise without some hope that these activities will bring them something valuable. In this light, it may make more sense to see the "escape" factor of the groups as being a necessary kind of help in the process of spiritual development. It is one phase of the withdrawal/ involvement cycle through which all people must pass, a time when distractions and demands are minimized so that clearer perceptions of reality can occur. These clearer perceptions then enable the individual to "re-enter" the daily world with renewed vigor and fresh direction. This may in fact be a rediscovery of the meaning of Sabbath.

This clearing of perception through a rhythm of silence and attentiveness is, as we see it, at the very core of contemplative practice. Our assumption is that to see the truth as it is, to perceive and respond to reality with diminishing preconception, prejudice and attachment, is to walk in closer harmony with the Will of God. And the ways in which such clearing of perception occur are the methods of prayer and meditation which constitute the "skillful means" of Eastern and Western traditions.

4

"Skillful Means"

Some Ways of Group Practice

Many great spiritual leaders of past and present seem to be trying to tell people that all one really needs to do to grow in spirit is to pray (or meditate), do the best one can in life, and walk in humility with God. The standards they set are as simple as their words. Certainly the message of the Christian Gospel can be seen as an exquisitely simple one. Christ died for our sins. All that is needed is to follow Him.

But modern Americans in search of spiritual grounding often cannot accept this degree of simplicity. They are convinced that there must be something more to it. There must be more to *do*. There must be some way of "learning how" to do it. This is the way most people find themselves at the beginning of pilgrimage. It is as if we have a great hunger for doing and for complexity, and it seems that hunger must to some extent be satisfied before we are able to proceed with humility and confidence. Thus "skillful means" become important.

There is perhaps no way to "do the best one can in life and walk in humility with God" except simply to do it. But there do seem to be ways of "learning how" to pray and to meditate. And there does indeed seem to be something which can be gained through repeated experiences with silence. Perhaps this is because almost all of our culture forces us away from silence, into ever-increasing levels of noise and activity. And because we habitually and mistakenly take silence to mean that something is wrong, blocked, or withdrawn. Therefore it makes sense to offer some practical teaching as to the "how to" of silence. In our first-year groups, this "how to" occupies the majority of many participants' time and interest throughout most of the year. They come with expectations that learning how to meditate will help them in some way, but they are often very unclear as to what meditation means or how one should go about it.

Therefore, we expose our first-year groups to what we have come to call a "cafeteria" of meditative approaches. We sample and experience approaches from classical Christian mysticism and from the contemplative traditions of the East. We try to stay with each approach for enough time to allow people to experience it in some depth, but we present a fairly wide variety. We do this in the hope that people will find some way or ways within this cafeteria which will feel natural, comfortable and sensible to their own individual needs. Thus we will present the open, formless meditations of Mahayana Buddhism, the visualizations of Tibetan traditions, the scriptural meditations of St. Teresa, the Chants of Hinduism, the silent mantras of Eastern Orthodox and Yogic traditions, the body movements of Sufism, the koans of Zen and many other approaches.

There is a danger of superficiality in this cafeteria-style of presenting skillful means, but we hope it is offset by an openness which will allow people with differing needs to find something of value, not requiring an arbitrary commitment to "one way and one way only." It is made clear to the participants that this is the purpose of the cafeteria approach, and that our expectations are that they will select one or two of the ways into which they can move more deeply and to which they can commit themselves more extensively. At the same time, there is an underlying assumption that the specific way in which one approaches prayer and meditation is not the most important thing. What is important is that prayer and meditation can become an integral and helpful part of one's life. Thus, while beginning group members are sampling and tasting various ways into silence, they are also gaining something far more important. They are gaining experience in being silent.

It is important in this not to let the technique overshadow the fact of silence. The different techniques tend to hold people's interest by offering new and exciting experiences. This adds some color and vitality to the pilgrimage, but it very easily can usurp the primary purpose of the group and turn the meditation experience into a form of entertainment. We have found it helpful to go ahead and enjoy the entertainment when it happens, but to keep conscious at the same time that what we seek lies well beneath and beyond the level of entertainment. Technique can too easily become an object for idolatry.

It would be wrong to say we present a complete spectrum of meditative approaches, for in fact most of the ways presented are ones which we have selected as being especially suited to integration with traditional Christian and Jewish orientations. The approaches of Christian mysticism clearly fall into this category, as does the Jesus Prayer of the Hesychasts, the formless quiet of the Quakers, and the candle meditations of Jewish mysticism. In addition, we draw heavily from the Mahayana Buddhist tradition, especially from Tibetan and Zen Buddhism. The Mahayana approach affirms other religious traditions, and has many elements which compare favorably with Christianity. For example, the Mahayana understanding of compassion relates very well to the Christian agapé, and the Buddhist idea of going beyond the illusion of self relates well to the Christian idea of "dying to be reborn," or, "losing oneself to find oneself." There are many other similarities,* but beyond the philosophical and theological understandings the most important offering of Mahayana Buddhism is its rich store of skillful means; ways of relaxation of body and mind, styles of concentration which cut through personal attachment and desire, and means of entering a very open and receptive silence which can be very helpful to Christians and Jews who wish to deepen their experience of prayer.

As indicated above, we have drawn from numerous other traditions as well, but the Christian and Mahayana contemplative approaches have carried the greatest emphasis. We have not done extensive work with methods of meditation which require effortful concentration (as in some yogic traditions), nor have we emphasized trance-like meditation. In general, the Mahayana influence coupled with a Judeo-Christian belief that God will have the ultimate say in how and when spiritual development is to occur has resulted in an emphasis on *open* silence. This means that the silence is generally not specifically focused, but rather consists of open, receptive waiting and listening, not trying to make anything happen, not trying to cling to anything or reject anything. This approach has been most helpful and seems to have a broader appeal than methods which are designed to achieve a certain kind of experience in meditation.

The most basic approach to meditation used by our groups consists of some preparatory breathing or stretching physical exercise, then sitting in a relaxed upright position and simply paying attention to what

---

*Tilden H. Edwards, "Criss-crossing the Christian-Buddhist Bridge," from RE-FLECTIONS OF MIND, Dharma Publishing, California, 1975.

happens within and around one. Sounds, thoughts, images and other
sensations are encouraged simply to come and go as they will, with no
extra attempt to label, analyze or otherwise meddle with them. Sometimes a chant precedes the silence as a way of "centering" attention. At
other times a silent mantra such as the Jesus Prayer or Sanskrit syllables
may be used as a base for attention during the silence. Counting the
breaths, simply watching, breathing or listening to sounds which occur
around one may also be bases for attention. When such bases for
attention are used, there is no attempt to concentrate forcefully or to
keep the mind from wandering. The mind is given permission to do
"what it wants," and the base for attention is simply there when the
individual feels he or she needs to do something with his or her attention.

We generally take an "apophatic" approach, assuming that the
sooner one gets beyond exciting or dramatic imagery in the silence, the
better. The highest priority is placed on silence in which one is acutely
aware of what the mind is doing at any given time, as well as of what is
going on around one, and when one can accept all that without struggle.
This may mean that the mind is quiet or noisy, calm or active. The
important thing is to watch carefully without interference. This approaches the Mahamudra style of Tibetan Buddhism and the beginning
of the contemplative phase of prayer as described in Christian mysticism, where one's perception of reality is not clouded by preoccupation
with personal desires and preconceptions.

Overall, an attitude of gentle permissiveness towards oneself is
encouraged. It is agreed that a certain amount of intentionality and effort
is necessary in order to schedule time every day for meditation and to sit
down to do it, but there the effort should stop. Once one has begun the
meditative practice, it is best if all trying and effort can cease. This
fosters the openly receptive state and discourages the vigorous mental
battles which often occur in more effortful approaches.

Prior to meditation, a period of physical exercise such as hatha yoga
is recommended. Similarly, deep and concentrated Yogic breathing will
be helpful at this time. The function of physical postures and breathing is
to relax and energize the body, which in turn helps relax and energize the
mind for meditation or contemplative prayer.

The periods of silence may be short (15 minutes or less) in very early
sessions of beginning groups, but are lengthened to approximately
twenty minutes within the first few weeks. In second-year groups the
time is usually extended to about 30 minutes and sometimes longer if the
group so desires. The Friday morning group, which has been in existence for four years at this writing, is now exploring extended periods of
silence based on a Zen style of 30 minutes of sitting followed by 10

minutes of slowly walking, followed by another 30 minutes of sitting. Usually the length of time spent in silence in the group is also the length of time recommended for the individual daily practice of the participants. On full or multiple day retreats, the silence might extend over the whole time.

In most group sessions, the leader keeps track of the time and ends the silence with soft clapping of his or her hands or the ringing of a small bell. After the silence is over, at least five minutes are given for people to stretch out, relax again, and slowly and gently prepare for some discussion. During this time there is an opportunity for people to make some notes in their journals. In general, a very slow and gentle transition is encouraged at the end of silence.

The group leader then usually asks if anyone has something to share, and some discussion begins. In beginning groups, the discussion usually centers around the experience of that particular period of silence, problems encountered with the practice, or experiences of the preceding week. Sometimes the leader will gently question people to help them clarify their experience, and sometimes other group members will relate to what is being said. This discussion period is usually quite open and unstructured, and simply consists of sharing and responding to whatever comes up.

In more experienced groups, there is less discussion about prayer or meditation techniques and experiences, and more talk about how contemplative spirituality does or does not integrate with ongoing daily life.

In addition to daily personal practice of prayer or meditation, beginning group members are usually asked to keep a "koan" in mind as they go through their daily living. These koans are not used in the full Rinzai Zen way of riddles with specific, set responses to be realized, but are rather simple thoughts or phrases which participants are asked to "plant" in their minds and to pay attention to whenever they can. Short scripture verses are often used, such as, "Be still, and know that I am God," or, "Our soul waits for the Lord." Usually a new "koan" is given every two to four weeks during a first-year group, and from time to time participants are asked to share any experiences or reflections they have had concerning this. Weight is placed on allowing an intuitive rather than analytical realization of the truth expressed by the phrase.

At times other "koans" are used which were learned from Tibetan Buddhism and serve to develop a fresh and clear perspective on mind and self-image. These usually take the form of questions such as, "Where do thoughts come from?", "What is the background behind my thoughts?" or, "Who am I?" These questions also sometimes serve as the basis for a specific approach to silence termed "analytic meditation."

In this form of meditation, the individual is asked to use the period of silence to observe his or her mind very closely and to experience where thoughts seem to come from, or to count his or her thoughts, or to look at the spaces between thoughts. In this experience, which many of our participants have found very revealing, a sense of "the observer" develops, namely that part of consciousness which seems to be watching the rest of the mind. The Tibetan Nyingma tradition encourages careful and direct examination of what makes up this "observer," how it does or does not interfere with the sequence of mental events, and how it differs, if it does, from the rest of the mind and from one's sense of self. A more iconoclastic form of analytic meditation is to focus on images of oneself, and to question the origin and substance of each of them as they arise. Such approaches to meditation are appropriate for first-year groups, but probably should not be presented until the group members have had some experience with less demanding forms of silence.

The "koans" to be kept in consciousness throughout the day help encourage another aspect of spiritual development practice which we strongly encourage. This is what in contemplative traditions is called "recollection," "mindfulness" or "witnessing." Here that impartial "observer" is encouraged to watch whatever is going on as the person goes through his or her daily life. It is a way of fostering immediate awareness of being. People are encouraged to begin this by quietly and simply noting whatever it is that they are doing while they are doing it. In the beginning it is helpful to say silently to oneself, "I am walking across the street," "I am doing the dishes," "I am driving the car," etc. With practice, this silent verbal comment can be dropped and the activity can be simply and subtly noted. This gentle encouragement of immediate awareness throughout the day constitutes another, more generalized form of meditation, and helps the individual not only realize his or her being more of the time, but also reveals a sense of the sanctity of every action and movement as each moment passes.

At the beginning of first-year groups, and as forms of evaluation from time to time thereafter, the members are asked to participate in a series of exercises and discussions which help to clarify how they perceive their spiritual journey and what they seem to need at present. These exercises and the format in which they are used have been compiled into an instrument called the "Self-Search Format" which is described in depth later in the book. We have found this format helpful not only in our long-term groups but in congregations and other groups where people are interested in becoming more clear about their spiritual needs.

In addition to the above methods of group activity and individual practice, nearly all our group members participate in at least one retreat during each year. At these retreats there is an opportunity for greater time in silence, the experience of more prolonged meditation exercises, and enhanced mindfulness. In addition to the usual chanting, visualization and other meditative approaches, the retreats normally include silent meals in which people are encouraged to watch their eating very carefully, and to pay close attention to the sights, sounds and other sensations around and within them as they eat. Also the retreats usually include some form of more intensive body work, such as movement to music and in silence with the sensations of the body being the base for attention (as opposed to fascination). Morning and evening prayer, Eucharist, and more extensive hatha yoga are usually included. Members also are encouraged to go on occasional retreats alone.

Finally, participants in long-term groups are encouraged to present or raise areas in which they are especially interested or which they would like to share with the group. Such presentations are usually given once a month at a longer meeting, and have included a wide variety of special interests such as fasting, mandalas, massage, music, psychology and spirituality, spirituality and social justice, liturgy, healing, etc. It is also during these long sessions that visiting spiritual leaders or representatives of differing traditions are invited to participate and share their experiences and perceptions.

In general, we schedule a day-long session for the first group meeting, using this time to go through the self-search format and explain scheduling and guidelines. Subsequent day-long meetings may be scheduled from time to time as needed during the course of the group. The group usually meets once a week for a minimum of two hours, and one of these meetings each month often is extended to three or preferably four hours. It is usually at these long meetings that new material is presented and time with spiritual friends is scheduled. The other three meetings during each month are normally used to work in greater depth on the material presented during the long session. This allows for regular input of new techniques and information, along with sufficient time to integrate and practice the material presented.

This schedule has varied from group to group, and would certainly have to be adapted to the specific needs of groups in other settings, but it can provide a helpful model for those who are thinking of setting up such a format.

We generally encourage beginning members to keep a journal in which they make notes of experiences and thoughts related to their pilgrimage. Some people have a lot of trouble doing this, but it is probably good to ask everyone at least to give it a try. It can be extremely helpful in clarifying one's perceptions at the time of writing, and can be very illuminating when reviewed after some period of time. The only important guideline concerning the journal is to use it as a tool for clarification and simple notation rather than as an attempt to intellectualize experience or to "figure out" what is happening.

There is one other primary aspect of "skillful means" which should be mentioned in the context of group activities. That is the role of the group leader in conducting discussion. This role should be one of helping the group members to *clarify* their perceptions of their experience. As mentioned before, participants seem to want to be told what to do, and they seem to want help in clarifying their thoughts, feelings and beliefs, but they do not want to be told what to think, feel or believe. In this regard, the most helpful thing a leader can do is to ask the kinds of questions which will help press each participant into clearer and more direct self-examination and clarification. These questions are generally non-judgmental. Ideally, they are very direct and basic questions which cut through assumptions and touch the most fundamental levels of perception. Often they sound like dumb questions. A few examples:

Participant: "I did not have a good meditation today."
Leader: "What is a good meditation?"
P: "One which is quiet and peaceful."
L: "What is it that you are trying to make peaceful?"
P: "My mind."
L: "Who is this 'me' that has your mind?"

P: "I had a wonderful experience in the silence today; great calm, and a feeling of peace and light."
L: "Were you aware of that feeling while you were having it?"
P: "Yes, I guess so."
L: "What part of you was making the judgment that it was wonderful?"

L: "What is the difference between prayer and meditation?"
P: "It seems like in prayer I have a real feeling of God's presence while in meditation I don't so much."
L: "What seems to *make* that difference? Why is that?"

P: "Today I felt a great feeling of love in the group."
L: "What does love feel like? Where does it seem to come from?"

Though these kinds of questions may at times sound corny or contrived, any honest attempt to answer them cannot help but raise deeper and deeper levels of exploration. In most of our groups, such questions are asked with a little grin and a little tongue-in-cheek. The participants know it is a kind of game, and will often ask the same kinds of questions of each other and of the leaders. But though it is a game, and hopefully one that can be handled lightly, it is important to try to answer the questions as honestly as possible. In this way the very roots of perception and self-image can be approached, and attachments and preconceptions can be loosened. The assumption here is that as preconceptions and rigid images are allowed to become more free, an underlying, inexpressable truth will begin to be seen.

Certainly the leader should not play the role of guru and respond only in terms of such pressing questions. The leader needs to share his or her own experience with frustrations, fears, understandings and ignorances in a direct and honest way, and should be free to make specific suggestions which may be of help in overcoming problems that participants may be having. All these suggestions, of course, need to be geared to the unique situation of each person.

Given this wide variety of approaches and concerns dealt with in groups, the steady awareness of the leader can be particularly important in helping groups avoid temptations of mere eclecticism, fascination, and ego-assertion. We have tried to cultivate leaders who care about keeping a steady eye on the underlying Simple Presence through all that is done, and who can leave room for others to begin cutting through the complications and heavinesses that block this awareness. Again, our leaders still are "on the way," and their awareness does falter many times. But the importance of the subtle way they hold the reins in such a group, or rather, the way they pay attention to the Holy Spirit's reins in the group, cannot be ignored.

The period of discussion time after silence is a very important one. It is here that people can share the fears they experience in prayer and meditation, and their (apparent) problems and triumphs. It is here that the support of the group for people's personal practice comes into full form. And it is here that one becomes able to feel somewhat less alone in one's pilgrimage.

5

Truth or Health?

The Relationship Between Psychology and Spirituality

One of the most common dilemmas which arise in beginning groups is the relationship between what is "spiritual" and what is "psychological." It is often very difficult for both members and leaders of groups to discern how to respond to issues which seem to be on the borderline between mind and spirit.

For example, let us say that one of the members of a beginning group is a young man who seems to be preoccupied with "psychological" issues. He can't seem to relate to the more "spiritual" concerns of others in the group. During the discussion periods after meditation, he describes the experiences he has had in the silence and attempts to analyze them for their psychological significance. "I saw an image of a man with an angry face," he says. "And I think it represented my father who was always angry with me." In describing his day-to-day experiences, he cannot seem to deal with their religious significance as do most of the other group members. Rather, he spends time talking about the troubles he is having with his family and co-workers. The group leaders are somewhat at a loss as to how to respond to this. They want to be open to this man, to meet him on his own ground, but at the same time they feel he is skewing the emphasis of the group discussions. Some of the other group members share this anxiety, and express the fear that "this will turn into group therapy." About all the leaders can do is continue gently attempting to re-direct the man's emphasis, asking questions such as, "Do you find that problem interfering with your prayer life?" or, "What do those concerns do to your awareness?"

But as time goes on, the man does not appear to be making any headway. The leaders are nearly convinced that he's simply in the wrong kind of group; that what he needs is therapy and not prayer.

Then one day something happens. After the silence, he says, "For the first time I really was able to see my feelings coming and going. And all those petty desires and fears I have . . . they just seemed to be taking place inside a small part of me. All the while, there was this sense of something deeper—something more constant, something which wasn't the least bit influenced by how I felt or what I wanted." This experience seems to reassure him deeply, and afterwards he is less preoccupied with his own psychology. He still has his problems, but they seem less awesome. Later he speaks of feeling more relaxed about some of his concerns, and he says that in being more relaxed he can take care of his problems with less ado. He also expresses an increasing interest in other people and a sense of deepening of his faith. He has been in touch with something bigger, deeper and more abiding than his personal concerns, and this has enabled some true sense of healing to take place.

As another example, there is a woman in a similar group who has always been very religiously active. She spends a good deal of time in church activities, has kept a personal prayer practice for many years, and is well-versed in the jargon of spirituality. The group leaders later learn that in addition to their group, she is involved in three other prayer groups, some of which meet more than once a week. She speaks easily of trusting in God, in the love of Christ, and in taking one's problems to the Lord in prayer. In her discussions after the silence she always tells of going to a "place filled with light" where she feels bathed in divine love. She never speaks of any fearful or uncomfortable experiences. She never seems to have any problems, but as others come to know her better they begin to sense that she is basically very lonely. She has few friends and is often at odds with her family. There is a kind of bitterness which emerges underneath her words, and she tends to be very disrespectful of anyone whose belief structure does not exactly fit with hers. She presses the other group members quite hard to try to have the same kinds of experiences she is having, seeming to want to validate herself through others. She feels that there is something "wrong" with the faith or practice of those who have different kinds of experiences.

After a while it becomes clear that to a large extent this woman has been using her spiritual practice to compensate for anger and bitterness, and to provide refuge from a life which holds little love or beauty for her.

The more time and energy she spends in contemplative practice, the more defensive she seems to become about herself. She is clinging to her faith and her practice so tightly that there is no room to be open to others of differing orientations. She is totally self-centered in her piety. The group leaders as well as the other participants begin to recognize this, but there is little that they can do. She completes a long-term group and then continues with her regular prayer meetings, and she is apparently none the wiser or freer as a result of her experience with the group.

In the first of these examples the young man tried to use spiritual practice in a psychological way. Just as the leaders were about ready to refer him for psychotherapy, he experienced some healing which lifted him above his psychological concerns and enabled him to proceed on his spiritual journey. In the second example, a woman who seemed totally unaware of her psychological difficulties retreated into a rigid spirituality and in spite of all attempts to encourage her self-confrontation, she appeared only to entrench herself more and more deeply in blindness. While both of these examples are fictitious, they are not unlike many of the situations which can be encountered in real-life experience, and they point out that everyone needs to look closely at the degree to which psychological and spiritual issues become mixed up in the process of contemplative practice.

With the recent rise in popularity of spiritual growth programs in the United States, and the increasing number of spiritual "fads" sweeping the country, such questioning becomes more and more important. Abuses and psychological distortions of spiritual practice are becoming increasingly obvious, and these bring about a healthy criticism and examination of spiritual programs. Many such programs have been labeled by critics as "quackery," "brainwashing," and "nothing more than empty promises for instant happiness." A prominent psychiatrist has recently proposed that an interest in mysticism arises when an individual fears his or her own aggressiveness. "Followers of mystical movements," he says, "wish to cancel the aggression of the world in order to do away with their own aggressive potential."* Such attempts to find psychodynamic causation for spiritual undertakings are not new. Freud himself saw nearly all religious activity as a defensive displacement of unconscious and unacceptable aggressive or sexual impulses.

In attempting to address these issues clearly and honestly the question of whether one is searching for truth or for health in spiritual practice becomes very important. One is compelled to ask: "Am I really

---

*Hartocollis, P., "Aggression and Mysticism," *Menninger Perspective*, Vol. 7, No. 4, Winter 1976-77. Menninger Foundation.

seeking to know God and to be in accordance with Divine Will, or am I looking for a way to ease some restlessness, pain or discomfort within myself?" When one feels a spiritual hunger, one must ask whether that hunger is the result of God's calling one forth to closer union, or whether it is a disguised sense of some psychological or interpersonal difficulty which calls for correction. In the first case, the search is for truth, for fulfillment in terms of seeing reality just as it is, and of being in harmony with that reality. In the second, the search is more for health, for the correction of a defect, for the remedy of something gone awry.

But how is one to know, in one's own heart, whether one's motives are "pure" or "unconsciously determined"? And in spiritual leadership, how is one to know what kind of guidance to give—psychological or spiritual? And what of the apparently vast conflicts between religion which sees a power beyond human beings, and psychology which generally does not? On the surface it seems it would require almost superhuman wisdom to discern whether a person needs spiritual help or psychological help. Truth and health have become so objectified and complex in our modern society that they seem almost totally unmanageable.

Our experience with Shalem has raised the possibility of simplifying this dilemma considerably. Through our own introspection and critique, we have come to question whether there really *is* any basic difference between psychological problems and spiritual problems. Perhaps, we suggest, truth and health are really one and the same thing. To be sure, most of us in the beginning entertained the assumption that psychology and spirituality were indeed two different fields of endeavor, dealing with two basically different aspects of human existence. Because of our acceptance of this dichotomy we were hoping to discover ways of *integrating* ideas and methods from both psychology and spirituality into a wholistic approach to human being. Those of us with psychological backgrounds tended to see spiritual experience as a psychologically motivated and determined phenomenon, to be explained in terms of identity, dependency, consciousness and anxiety. Those with more theological backgrounds tended to see psychology as a basically spiritual phenomenon, one of the many gifts God has given to humankind. But nearly all of us saw the two fields as different, and in need of some kind of integration.

We struggled for quite some time to move in the direction of such integration.* We involved ourselves in diligent, careful and rather extensive processes of thinking *about* psychology and spirituality in the hope

---

*Gerald G. May, "A Spiritual Gift and an Offering in Return: Spiritual Awareness and Western Psychology," Alban Institute, Washington D.C., 1975.

of generating concepts which would unify the two fields. While we accumulated many valuable learnings and interesting conceptual models in this process* our most valuable learning may have been that we were going about dealing with the problem in altogether the wrong way.

We had assumed that spirituality and psychology were basically different phenomena which needed to be unified by a new way of thinking. Now it appears more likely that psychology and spirituality *are in fact only different ways of THINKING ABOUT one basic reality*.

If our sense of this is true, then to try to integrate the concepts would be only an exercise in mental gymnastics. It would be much more reasonable to try to cut through the concepts altogether, ease our habitual desire to think *about* reality, and see if we can perceive the uncluttered and common truth which lies beneath the concepts of *both* psychology and spirituality. Such an approach is at the very heart of contemplative spirituality. It is a process of watching reality very carefully, directly and immediately, being willing to be involved in it just-as-it-is, without window dressing or prejudice. Out of this kind of perception seems to come a sense that truth and health are in fact the same thing.

To understand this more fully, one needs to consider that a person's "psychology" inevitably has to do with three basic things. First, it has to do with one's awareness; its quality, its contents, its clarity. Second, it has to do with one's images of oneself and the world around one; the good or bad values placed on those images, their stability, and the degree to which they approximate reality. Third, it has to do with the way in which one's desires and fears impinge upon one's feelings and behavior; how much of behavior is determined by personal desire and fear, or how free the individual is from these attachments.

At core, these are the same three things which seem to determine the degree to which an individual can perceive the truth as-it-is. Awareness must be full and clear. One's images of self and others must be free enough not to cloud accurate perception. And desire and fear must not be so strong as to impede one's ability to accept reality as it is.

In this light, the search for truth need be no different from the search for health; the raw bases of spirituality and psychology are one and the same thing. This understanding is well spelled-out in the literature of a variety of Eastern and Western contemplative traditions, in which the message seems to be that as one moves more and more deeply into the direct experience of consciousness, all the events of mind and emotion are seen simply as differing manifestations of a common consciousness.

---

*Gerald G. May, THE OPEN WAY, Paulist Press, New York, 1977.

There is something potentially reassuring about this understanding. What it means is that one need not concern oneself with great diagnostic struggles about oneself or others. Beneath the clutter of emotions and conceptualizations, we are simply asking, "Who are we? Who is God? What are we here for? and How should we live our lives?"

But as comforting as this understanding may be, one must be careful in its application. It might be tempting, for example, to say "Well, if psychological problems and spiritual problems are basically the same, then all one needs to do is work hard on one's spiritual development and seek after that common Absolute which underlies everything." The mistake in this statement is that it again makes the dichotomy between spirituality and psychology. It says, in effect, work on spirituality and don't worry about psychology. This can lead to a feeling that meditation, prayer or other spiritual techniques are all that is needed to respond to any problems one may have. Which is just as absurd as saying that psychoanalysis is the one way to God.

The hazard lies in the polarity itself rather than in choosing one side over the other. When one is caught up by the duality of spirit—vs.—psyche, one is indeed liable to try to pit one against the other or to disguise one as the other. But the answer to this is not to try to re-determine which is which. The answer lies in maintaining one's attentiveness throughout, continuing to clear one's mind of such distinctions. If this can happen there need be no conflict, and distortions will be automatically avoided.

There is nothing in this that says one should not question one's motivations or that one cannot be cognizant of and responsive to one's emotions during the course of contemplative practice. Similarly, there is no reason why one cannot find "something spiritual" on the analyst's couch. The only question is whether one can continue to be open, attentive, and receptive. A wholistic approach to human beings does not have to be created—things are wholistic just as they are. There only needs to be room in one's mind to realize this, and to recognize when one has been caught up in one side or the other of the mind/spirit dichotomy.

Thus, prospective leaders of spiritual development groups need not become overly concerned with figuring out the vicissitudes of mind and spirit. In the course of the group some "psychological" problems may surface which need to be handled psychologically. Other "psychological" problems may surface and experience immediate healing. "Spiritual" experiences may turn out to be "psychological" and vice versa. Through it all, the members and the leadership should simply try to be aware of what's happening and maintain their attentiveness while responding as needed. Nothing more complex need be made of it.

Lest this sound terribly oversimplified, let me describe some of my own experiences with the process. When I began work with spiritual development groups, I was very conscious of different psychological "quirks" in myself and in those with whom I worked. These "quirks" could be anything from a previously repressed feeling of anger which suddenly came into consciousness, to a destructive habit of talking too much, to deep anxieties or depression. Whenever I would identify one of these difficulties in myself or someone else, it seemed I had to go through some rather complex attempt to respond to it. Something was wrong and needed to be fixed. Then the inevitable question always arose: What should we do about it? Sometimes it seemed that the answer might lie in a different approach to meditation or prayer; some new spiritual technique. At other times it seemed that what was required was some psychological exploration. At still other times it seemed that the best approach was simply to pray for mercy. All of these choices seemed, and in fact *were*, reasonable at the time. What was not so reasonable was that I felt there was some conflict between them. If I took the route of prayer, for example, it somehow seemed that I was denying or derogating the value of psychological understanding. And vice versa.

This is really an absurd point of view. It has dawned on me more recently to ask, "What is wrong with simply doing what needs to be done?" There is no reason to feel that in responding to a certain problem one must somehow engage in conflict between differing schools of thought or different perceptions of reality. Such conflictual issues only come up when one tries to mold reality into a conceptual understanding. Now it seems far more sensible to try to see whatever the problem is very clearly, and then simply to respond to it in the best way one can. Once again, where there was what seemed to be inpenetrable complexity there is now an awesome and almost terrifying simplicity. I want to ask, "Is there nothing more?" "It seems like there has to be something extra—*something in addition*—something I can struggle with." But as I search for that something extra, I realize again that I am just creating more problems for myself and for those with whom I work. Out of this understanding has come a phrase which reflects what may be my most basic perception of psychological and spiritual reality: *"It's only complicated if you try to figure it out."*

Sometimes someone may need some psychotherapy. And sometimes someone may need to meditate a little more or a little less. And sometimes someone may need to spend some time and energy in helping others, examining conscience, or something else. All we can do is pray for guidance, try to see the situation as clearly as possible and maintain our attentiveness while responding in the best way we know how.

It might be thought that my psychiatric training helped minimize my fears about potential problems in the groups. But in fact, this training actually increased my anxieties. Having seen first the almost infinite number of ways in which the human mind can befoul itself, there was no end to the terrible fantasies I could concoct. It was in truth only a sense of prayerful reverence which enabled me to maintain my attentiveness, and indeed there were plenty of times when this too failed me.

The accounts of other group leaders who have little or no psychological training have mirrored my experience very closely. While we all have anxieties about this area, we have also all found that the one thing really needed is prayerful, open attentiveness.

Even though one may recognize that the psychology/spirituality dichotomy is at core false, and even though one may develop some trust that prayerful attentiveness is the basis for dealing with problems in this area, there is still a need for some way of understanding the vicissitudes of mind and of human behavior. Since a large part of contemplative practice involves confronting one's own mental and emotional experience very directly, it is not surprising that most contemplative traditions have developed a kind of "spiritual psychology," by means of which some understanding can occur.

"Spiritual Psychology"

We are all aware of what is called "mind," though most of us would be hard put to define it. We are also all aware of a sense of "self," which is similarly difficult to define. Most contemplative traditions relate mind and sense of self very closely to consciousness, and an integral part of contemplative spiritual development is the exploration and clarification of mind, self-sense, and consciousness. This is consonant with much of Western thinking, of both psychological and theological forms. The major difference in the contemplative approach, however, is its emphasis that exploration of mind, self and consciousness can best take place through *direct experience and immediate observation*, as contrasted with objective analysis and conceptualization. More simply stated, the emphasis is more on the *experience of* and less on *thinking about*.

It is to be expected that this emphasis on the direct experience of consciousness would emerge from a tradition which relies heavily on silence. Contemplative prayer and meditation absolutely force the direct experience of consciousness to occur. In turn, this results in inevitable confrontation of "psychological" phenomena. While in some modern

Western approaches to prayer the experience of personal mental events may be seen as an obstacle to communion with God and labeled as "distractions," in many contemplative traditions such experiences are used as material for growth. They constitute a kind of fertile ground in which growth can take place. It is assumed that if one is to allow the ground to be cleared for an unaltered perception of the truth, one must first have some knowledge of *how* one perceives that truth, *who* it is that is perceiving, and *what* the mechanisms of that perception really are.

Thus, an important aspect of any contemplative practice can be the direct experience of mind, consciousness and self-image. It is important to understand that in the exploration of consciousness here, it is not just the *contents* of consciousness which are studied, but the nature and quality of consciousness itself. The individual is encouraged to watch his or her mind very carefully during periods of silence. Questions are asked which encourage this ability to watch. For example, one may be asked to count one's thoughts for a minute or two. Then to see if one can sense the quality of the spaces between thoughts or the background upon which thoughts seem to occur. One also watches to see how thoughts arise, where they seem to come from and where they seem to go. When the ability to observe one's mind in this way is developed, the person is asked to try to see who it is that is watching the mind. What is the nature of this "observer?"

This process questions the very essence of self-image. What is there within this directly experienced consciousness which seems to be "me?" What makes it up? How does it come into prominence and then fade from view? What influences it, and how does it seem to change from one moment to the next?

In our groups, such practices have been found to be very helpful in assisting people to develop an increasingly clear sense of the relationship between one's image of oneself and one's image of God; the various obstacles and confusions which seem to get "in the way" of prayer, and the desires and attachments which cloud daily life.

There is little attempt to push for a logical explanation of the phenomena encountered during such practice, and most of the emphasis is placed on learning-through-experience at a deep and intuitive level. However, credibility is given to naturally occurring attempts at rational explanation. It is assumed that we know the world *both* through experience and reason, and that *both* of these faculties need to be affirmed in any approach which attempts to be wholistic.

Emerging from this practice is an increasing sense that there is a difference between reality as-it-is and one's images *of* reality. This applies to one's images of God, of the world, of other people, and of oneself. This helps to build an accurate understanding of the obstacles which lie in the path of spiritual development.

The root of these obstacles is terror. As one moves into the depths of silence and contemplation, there are many layers of fear which need to be traversed. At a superficial level, there is a fear of loss of control which accompanies the necessary relaxation and the relinquishing of usual preconceptions and prejudices. This fear of loss of control may be experienced in many ways: fear of going "crazy" or of becoming vulnerable to destructive influences within oneself or others, or of being abandoned without one's usual hand-holds on "reality."

After the fear of loss of control there is usually a fear of loss of self in one form or another. At first this may be associated with various aspects of self-image which are discovered to be false or impermanent. "Perhaps I am not basically a good person." "Maybe I'm not as good at interpersonal relationships as I'd thought." "Perhaps I don't have as much of a handle on my life and my faith as I had hoped," etc. Later, the fears about self-image become even more critical as times are experienced when self is not defined at all. While such experiences are usually seen as very beautiful, they are also riddled with underlying anxiety, for when one ceases to define oneself, one experiences the possibility of not being. This begins the direct confrontation of "losing oneself to find oneself" or of "dying to be reborn"; the absolute terror of spiritual truth.

In conjunction with the experience of these fears, there is also an exposure to the many defenses and resistances which one throws up against spiritual growth; the clinging to aspects of will, control and self-image, the attachment to gratification of personal desire, the hunger for omnipotence, and the basic struggling with God over whose will is going to be done.

All these fears are encountered in one form or another no matter what kind of contemplative practice is employed. And in one way or another it is important to allow people to grow through their experience of these fears at their own rate. If through pressure from leaders, peers, or themselves, they press on through contemplative darkness faster than their ability to cope, their minds and spirits are likely to become bruised. Even more likely, they will become defensive about the entire enterprise of spiritual development, turning their backs on it in terror.

Thus, it is very important that group leadership or individual spiritual direction communicate an attitude of gentleness and permissiveness, encouraging people to pay attention to their own internal signals about how far they should go along a certain track at any given time.

It can be seen from this way of describing what happens to self-image that the net effect is one of loosening one's grip on that image; recognizing it *as* an image, taking it less and less seriously. This is consonant with our impression that one of the factors characteristic of spiritual growth is a decreasing sense of self-importance, and in its place, a growing open compassion for others and humility in the face of God. But along the path of this development, there are innumerable ups and downs. Often self-importance creates a backlash after it has become threatened in some spiritual practice or experience. Then, for a while, the individual may experience even greater extremes of selfishness and self-interest. What may appear to the individual as selfless behavior may in fact turn out to be a subtle but very treacherous selfishness, such as feeling "holier than thou."

Such ups and downs can be minimized if the setting is one in which there is no pressure to move at a pace faster than that with which one feels comfortable. It is also helpful for members of a spiritual development group to share, with the group as a whole or with their "spiritual friend," the varied positive and negative experiences they are having along the way. Besides providing some objective clarification of the process, this often helps them take the whole business less seriously. Some of the heaviness is lifted, especially if humor can be seen amidst the drama of private experience.

Many "psychological" phenomena surface during the course of silence. The practice of contemplative prayer makes this inevitable. In a state of quiet relaxation, old memories and feelings come to consciousness. Previously unknown assumptions and prejudices may surface unannounced. Tears and giggles erupt without warning. When such experiences are shared openly, the attitude of the leadership becomes very important. If such feelings and responses are met with an attitude of heaviness, seriousness and anxiety, the group as a whole as well as the individual involved may become preoccupied with "making a big deal" of them. When this happens, it is very easy for the entire group to lose its openness and attentiveness. It is therefore important that the leaders recognize that such events, however dramatic, tragic, painful or meaningful they may seem, are simply releases of certain aspects of self-image and do not need to be analyzed or fixed. They should be handled with respect but lightly, like the distractions they are. This is not to stifle them, but simply to let them be what they are and not to make anything extra out of them.

It is well known that certain spiritually oriented groups engage in what might be called extremes of bizarre or hysterical behavior. Screaming, crying, convulsing, going into trances, etc., are all things which are popularly associated with spiritual groups of one kind or another. The thought of such occurrences is often enough to make a prospective group leader flee in panic. In our experience with Shalem, such things just don't happen. Tears come sometimes, as do giggles and strange mind and body sensations. Psychic phenomena are sometimes encountered. But nobody goes berserk. The reason for this, I think, is that over-dramatization is not encouraged. Nothing special is made of a few tears. Psychic events and weird internal sensations are dealt with as calmly as possible. People are encouraged to accept such experiences just as they are, neither dramatizing nor minimizing them.

To summarize, our basic understanding of the relationship between psychology and spirituality is that they are different approaches to a common reality, therefore requiring no special integration except from a purely conceptual standpoint. In spite of this, the "psychological" aspects of "spiritual" development remain the source of a good deal of anxiety both for participants and leaders who are "beginners" in contemplative practice. The basic method of handling spiritual and psychological problems which may arise in the course of contemplative practice is to see what is happening as clearly as possible and then simply and prayerfully respond in the best way one can.

6

"By Their Fruits You Shall Know Them"

Contemplative Practice and Social Responsiveness

We have already spoken of the importance of recognizing one's place in history and community if one is to avoid alienation and narcissism in spiritual growth. In practice, awareness of one's location in the community of humankind is insufficient by itself. If one is truly open to that awareness, one is forced to confront *how one responds to that community*.

Meditation and contemplative prayer invariably raise the age-old questions of whether one is enriching one's life or escaping from it; whether one is preparing for greater service or being selfishly introspective. Even before I began work with Shalem I remember many instances in which people would share these kinds of suspicions with me. One woman said "I just don't trust that meditation business. It's like sitting in a cave and contemplating your belly button while the rest of the world goes hungry."

Another woman spoke of her teenage daughter who had joined an exclusive religious cult.

> I can't even communicate with her anymore, now that she's into this religious thing. She's stopped studying her school work. She says things like "If God wants me to pass that exam, I will. If He doesn't. I won't." I believe in God too, but I believe you've got to work at some things yourself in this life.

Similar concerns have come up in our own groups. A very common fear was expressed by a man who said:

All of this meditation and contemplation practice keeps emphasizing that you should relax and let go. I feel like I'm learning how to let go and it feels good, but it also worries me. I feel much freer about things than I used to—things like success and failure and whether somebody likes me or not. Stuff like that just doesn't seem to bother me very much anymore. I like that, but it scares me too. When does it stop? Am I just going to go on letting go until I don't care about anything anymore? Am I going to become insensitive to other people's needs, am I going to become so lackadaisical that I lose my job and my security? And how can I be sure that if I try to give over to God's will that God's will will actually be done? How can I be certain that I'm not just substituting laziness for caring?

These are very real and important questions, and it is vital that people be allowed to ask them. But there are no easy answers. If one searches for answers in religious writings one nearly always encounters paradox. Jesus speaks of "letting go" when he tells us to "take no thought for the morrow," or to "forsake your parents" or to pray "Thy will be done." But just as often he tells us to love our neighbors, do good for those who despise us and obey the law. He touches our sense of responsibility with the story of the good Samaritan, and then our sense of total acceptance with the story of the prodigal son. Such apparent paradoxes are just as common in the Old Testament and in the scriptures of Hinduism, Buddhism and Islam. In fact, the paradoxes often go deeper, for it is often *through* letting go that one is prepared to love and respond to one's neighbor.

In essence, modern spiritual pilgrims are faced with a triple dilemma. First the scriptures seem unclear, often even contradictory in explaining to what extent one should try to do good and how much one should simply let be. Second, one's friends, family and society are often very suspicious and mistrustful of what's going to happen as one goes deeper into contemplative practice. It often seems that they are watchful, even waiting for one to demonstrate self-centeredness by "copping out" from responsibility or using religion as an escape. The structure of Sabbath no longer exists to provide an acceptable rhythm for contemplation and action. Third, in one's own mind one is seldom really clear as to what it is that can or should determine responsible behavior. If I decide to do a "good" thing, is that because it's good and needs doing, or because God guides me to do it, or because of some egoism that motivates me to feel self-satisfied if I do it?

All three of these problems revolve around one basic issue, namely how one perceives one's self in relation to the world and to God. While the end goal of most contemplative spirituality is a realization of oneness with the ultimate power of the universe, the fact is that most people, most of the time, feel separate from that ultimate power and from the rest of the world. And as long as they do, they are forced into questions of individual will and sinfulness. It is that separation which makes a person feel he or she must decide what is good and then do it. The trouble here is that one may experience great difficulty in deciding what is truly good or bad.

Nearly everyone who has participated in our groups has been aware that many behaviors which appear to be altruistic and charitable are really quite selfish. It always seems that one's motives are very suspect. For example, one woman said:

> I try to do good in all things. I try to act in a loving way towards everyone. I give money to charities. I volunteer my time in a nursing home. But I'm doing these things because I think I *ought* to do them; because I'd feel guilty if I didn't do them.
>
> And sometimes I wonder if that isn't just serving myself. I'm certain that what I'm doing isn't really selfless, because I feel a kind of sticky pride about it—and I even sometimes find myself thinking of myself as a better *person* than those who aren't so openly charitable. Lord knows whether what I do is really good or not. I mean, how can I know whether the money I give really goes to help people or whether it goes to keep the charity business operating? And how do I know whether acting in a loving way towards people is really what's best for them? Maybe sometimes it would be better for them if I yelled and screamed at them . . . I'm just not wise enough to know what's really good or bad.

This is, of course, a very old religious problem. Yet it never seems quite so pressing or quite so special as when one encounters it in the course of contemplative practice. For in contemplative practice one spends time confronting one's own mind, and if one never previously doubted the reliability of one's thought processes, contemplative practice will insure that one does.

Sitting quietly in prayer or meditation, one sees the mind going through its erratic and disorganized hi-jinks. Childish at one moment, tragic the next, prideful, clinging, longing, selfish, rigid and frightened, the mind seems to reveal no true consistency—no solid substance which can be relied upon. The possibility of trusting this mind to decide issues of morality or ethics seems increasingly questionable, and one becomes increasingly aware of one's innate susceptibility to sin.

This experience comes as a mixed blessing to most of the people who have participated in our groups. On the one hand, people are often relieved to discover that no matter how hard they work at "figuring out" how to live their lives they will not be successful. Sensing that the answer must then come from somewhere else, one can breathe a little sigh at not having to try so hard to manage every aspect of one's existence. On the other hand, there is often considerable anxiety about where the answer *will* come from, or even if it will come. One begins to sense that one's previously held concepts and images of "the" way life should be are little more than that: concepts and images. And one is forced to wonder where the truth can be found.

But answers do seem to come. The true blessing is that in moments of quiet and openness one does encounter hints of what for the lack of better words can be called truth. These glimpses more than anything else provide reassurance and confidence for both continuing personal contemplative practice and doing what one can in response to the needs of others. Such transient perceptions of truth are very difficult to describe in words, and yet nearly everyone has experienced them.

One woman described it in this way:

> I'd been trying to decide what to do with my life. It seemed that so many of my activities were meaningless—just things to pass the time. I wanted to do something that would really help people, but I didn't know what. I tried to figure it out but the things I wanted to do seemed selfish and the things I thought I *should* do seemed boring. Then one day this sense just came to me that what I needed to do was just go ahead with my life as it is unfolding—to take each moment and live it as clearly and fully as I can—and that's all. Right then it seemed that if I did that, selfishness and boredom wouldn't even enter into it—that selfishness and boredom are just reactions I have to life; thoughts *about* life that have nothing to do with living.

Another woman said:

> I was feeling very guilty about taking too much time for myself away from my family. And I was feeling guilty that I wasn't doing enough for all the people in the world who don't have it as good as I do. It was like I needed to do something different, but I was pulled in several directions at once. I prayed about it a little, and I worried about it a lot, but it always seemed unresolved. Then this morning while I was just sitting drinking my coffee, it all made sense. I could see it all happening and—I don't know—I just feel easier about it. It's like now I can be free to do what's best at any given time—I don't have to worry at it and figure it out. It's like I can trust something—is it God? I don't know. All I know is that it's clear—it's sure.

A man gave the following account:

> I work in government and there are always things going on that I feel ambivalent about: dishonesty and treachery and selfishness. Pettiness. There are times when I want to become very righteous and indignant and make sure

that everything I do is scrupulously right. But I can't function that way. I mean people and governments and administrations just aren't that pure. And I certainly don't want to go about being "holier than thou." Well, I don't know, but somehow it came clear to me that what I need to do is just do the best I can and not make too big a deal of it. I used to take pride in doing something right and I would feel guilty if I cheated a little on something. But now it seems that neither guilt nor pride have a rightful place in my life—all I can do is the best I can do. I like that feeling, but it scares me a little.

These perceptions are very simple, general things. None of them came as mystical visions or forceful callings. Rather, they are deep sensations that in living one's life clearly and fully in the best way one can, one is somehow in harmony with things. More importantly, these sensations were perceived as being true and undeniable at the time they were experienced. They did not appear in the heat of some passion or craving, but in quiet. None of them seem very dramatic or special. No one got a zealous sense of mission. No one went forth proclaiming that they were doing the will of God and challenging the structure of the world. In fact, all of these insights seem rather mundane, simple, and common-sensical.

In the last analysis we cannot say for certain that perceptions like these are accurate revelations of truth. They remain subject to testing in life, to critique, to re-evaluation. But we *can* say that each individual felt they were the truest perceptions they had experienced at the time. People do have a sense of what is true and what isn't. When one feels that one's eyes are open, that one is not shutting things out or pulling oneself this way or that but is relaxed and open to things as they are, and when one then feels something that harmonizes with one's deepest percep-tions, then one comes away with a sense that the truth has indeed been touched. For most people, this sense of rightness holds more credibility than something one has worked out logically yet which somehow feels wrong. Again, everyone can be misled, and it is always necessary to check perceptions out against prior personal and historical experience, against other people's perceptions, and against their application in daily life. But for most of our participants, most of the time, insights such as these do seem to stand up against every test. There is something deep in them, something solid and simple and irrevocable.

With repeated experiences such as these, people tend to grow into a more secure trust in the Divine Power of life. There seems to grow within them an openness to things as-they-are, and a relaxing of attempts to master destiny through the power of one's own will. If a person who has reached this point of trust is asked whether he thinks he's doing his own will or the will of God, he may be struck by the fact that he hasn't really been worrying about it too much. In attempting to respond logically, he may say something like "I don't really know. I hope and pray that I'm doing God's will, but who am I to say?" And if one asks him to explain how his decisions are made, he might say "I don't become so caught up in this or that—something needs doing and I do it. I don't take any great pride in it, for I'm just doing whatever I can. But I don't feel guilty either, for I'm living my life the best way I know how."

What can be seen under these answers is that this person is not struggling so much with issues of "My will or Thine." In fact there seems to be very little concern about self at all. What we may presume has happened is that this individual has become less self-interested, less self-conscious, and less self-centered. On the face of this description it might appear that there is a loss of caring, or of concern for others. But the caring and concern are there. *It's just that they are no longer manifested so much in how the person describes himself as in what he actually does.* And this can be ascertained only by being in this person's presence for a while.

Nearly everyone has met someone who fits this description. Someone who no longer struggles with his or her life but who seems to live it simply, undramatically, yet fully. Someone who doesn't make a big deal out of himself or herself, but who simply responds to you as you are. Someone who doesn't fully fit your preconceptions of what a "good" person should be, but who you know simply *is* good. There are many such people in the world, and they don't seem to fit in any stereotype. They can be found in all occupations and situations. Whatever they do, they just do it, accumulating no great fanfare or misery unto themselves, yet somehow radiating compassion and love.

It is always helpful to remember someone like this, to have the direct knowledge of what such people are like. It helps one rest a little more easily with the fears one has about one's own future. No number of words or concepts can substitute for the knowing of such a person.

Though contemplative practice may involve a great deal of what appears to be self-centered introspection, its final goal is always a diminishment of self-importance. And though it may appear at times to be a dramatic or even heroic undertaking, the legitimate outcome of contemplative practice is very simple, very ordinary, and nothing special. For some people it may be necessary to go through a rather extensive and turbulent period of self-searching and spiritual turmoil before simplicity and clarity can emerge. For others such drama is only a hindrance. For still others it will unfortunately be an enticing seducer which calls the individual into ever-increasing self-importance. The final sacrifice of this drama is one of the most difficult events in spiritual growth. There are times when one feels very empty, devoid of color and excitement; times when contemplative practice seems terribly boring and unedifying. These may be the most precious times of all, for it is through them that one's attention can turn away from self-entertainment and towards the simple beauty of life just-as-it-is. And it is through them that the true mystery of social responsiveness emerges. One is no longer *apart from* others, doing things *to or for* them. One is somehow living *in unity with* others, acting out of a deep organic relatedness, participating fully in the growth and healing of humanity.

In the second year of the study group which produced this book, we had a meeting in which we discussed these issues. The question was "How can we know that what we're doing in contemplative practice is leading us to better lives—towards more concern and benefit to our fellow human beings?" In the course of the discussion we spoke of good and evil, and how to decide which was which. We talked about how to rid ourselves of the demons inside us. Parker Palmer said "What I think is that you've got to make it so boring inside that the demons simply lose interest in being there." We all laughed, but at the same time we realized that there was something there that made a lot of sense—that maybe it indeed is through ordinariness, simplicity and downright dullness that the seductive forces of self-service finally pass into unimportance.

Another conclusion that evening was that it is impossible to establish arbitrary standards of good and evil which can guide all of one's behavior. In the last analysis, mature moral action must come through one thing: *clear vision*. It is only when one's perception of the world is freed from the clouds of prejudice, preconception and imagery that truly moral behavior can spring forth. The more clearly and accurately one can see things just-as-they-are, the more consonant one's behavior will be. This is also the basic tenet of how contemplative practice leads to ethical behavior. It assumes that one way towards clarity of vision is through contemplative practice—that meditation, quiet prayer and daily mindfulness are ways we can participate in cleansing our vision.

There is something frighteningly simple about this approach. Sometimes it feels as though one were taking a great risk in sacrificing one's hold on preconceptions of good and evil. But the risk is probably not as great as imagined. There is nothing in this approach that says one should *destroy* one's images, preconceptions and prejudices. Only that one not cling to them so tightly. This is one of the very important lessons of contemplative practice. The "letting go" of preconceptions does not mean to destroy them. It means only that one ease one's grip on them so that there can be space within and around them. It is within this space that clarity of vision can occur. In fact, sometimes in acting out one's images of what is right, striving for one's ego sense of justice, the primacy of ego can be defeated. The safeguard here is one of *humility*; knowing and affirming that one does *not* have access to ultimate truth, but striving for what one feels to be right in the best way one can. Humility means that one can accept oneself as one is without clinging too desperately to one's preconceptions and images, and thus be willing to take the risk of action.

When our study group began to deal with the question of whether contemplative practice leads to greater moral behavior we assumed we could answer simply by evaluating whether our participants were becoming more or less involved in social service. But immediately we were confronted by the same problem with which the participants themselves had to deal. How do we judge what constitutes moral behavior? Social action itself cannot be an adequate index without establishing arbitrary standards of what constitutes good social action and bad social action. It seems the only way to approach the question is to examine the subjective experience of participants as well as their behavior, to look for compassionate perceptions as well as actions, and to look for changes in self-importance.

It does seem that most of our group members begin their participation in a relatively self-interested frame of mind and that their attention remains more on themselves than on others for a considerable period of time. At least in terms of their verbalizations in the groups themselves, this seems to be the case. Then, at some point, there begins to be a broadening of interest, a deepening concern for others. In terms of actual behavior, some of our participants report finding themselves evolving into greater social action and commitment to community, but for others the reverse is true.

For example, one person began contemplative practice at a point in his life when he was very much involved in social action projects. He was a member of several groups dedicated to social, economic and ecological improvement. He spent a good deal of time with troubled people, counseling and helping them in the best way he could. After a couple of years of contemplative practice, he found himself less involved in these kinds of activities. But he was also aware that his prior investment in these activities had been a tight, driven, almost obsessive engagement. He did them because he thought he ought to do them. He did them because he'd feel guilty if he didn't.

Looking back now, he is not certain how much good it all actually accomplished. He is aware that his activities *looked* good on the surface—that he could have presented an impressive accounting of his behavior to anyone who wanted to judge him, but he is uncertain as to how much real human help came from all his efforts.

Now he has a different attitude:

> Before, I would see someone who needed help, and that person would be a kind of object for me—something I wanted to influence or change. Now I look at a person and I simply feel that person is me. We are one in all of this. People are no longer objects. Sometimes it seems I *do* less, but I certainly feel more, resonate more deeply with others.

In spite of all the moral questions concerning the validity of behavior, it is possible to say that people in our groups, presumably as a result of contemplative practice, do tend to experience a kind of transformation of social consciousness. That transformation seems to lead away from generalized stereotypes of helping others, and towards more open compassion and sensitivity to things and people as they are. The direction of this transformation was well described by the man we just quoted. He began with the thought "I should help that person," and moved toward the sense "That person is me." Again, one cannot blindly assume simply because a person *feels* some resonance with others that this means he or she will respond helpfully. The true spiritual question here is perhaps more "What is really needed *by* the others?" rather than "How do I feel about them?" If I am hungry, perhaps it is more important, right now, today, that you feed me than that you feel for me. Feelings of resonance, or even of identity with others are simply an early stage of spiritual growth. They still need to be supplemented by a motivation to *respond*. It is only when one reaches that idealized stage of actually *being one with* all others that responses spring fully and immediately from the situation at hand with no additional need for motivation.

As a case in point I can describe some changes which have taken place in myself in this regard. As a therapist I began with the image that my clients needed my help, and that I needed to give them something of myself in order to help them. At the end of a day of counseling I would feel tired, drained of energy. And many of my clients came to feel dependent upon me and therefore less secure within themselves.

Now, I hold the image of helping clients less tightly. I am more simply with them. I feel their pain and joys even more deeply, often as if they were indeed my own, but at the same time I am less pressured to *do* something for them. I am no longer drained at the end of the day. Instead of *giving to*, I have *resonated with*, and it seems very clear that the clients do better. They feel better about themselves. I am still a very important person to them, but few if any feel they would crumble without me. I realize that all of this change cannot be attributed to contemplative practice. Many therapists experience movements in this direction simply through maturation and experience. However at a subjective level, I am convinced that much of the change is so deeply related to my contemplative practice that I could not separate the two. Perhaps more basically, I now have a deep conviction that I do not do the healing of anyone. I find myself praying for my clients, and watching in simple awe as something beyond me works within them towards health. But much of the time I must still base my actions and responses on what I sense to be "right." I must continue to struggle with right and wrong behavior.

Many people in our groups have experienced similar kinds of changes in their relationships with families, spouses, congregations and society at large. Again, the absolute goodness or badness of such a change cannot be evaluated at this point. And for most people, it may even be dangerous to try to rely totally on an *image* of resonating with other people and responding to intuitive senses about what to do or not do. The problem here is that our image of the role of clear vision in determining moral action may not be quite correct. One cannot know this *until* one's vision is truly clear. In the meantime, then, it is important not to discard or derogate one's sense of moral justice. Even though that sense may be tinged with many unconscious self-serving distortions, it still remains the best guideline one has for what needs to be done. And even though it may be clouded with many "shoulds" and "oughts" against which we might want to rebel, it will at least get us moving in response to the daily pain and suffering of others around us. To remain inactive, insensitive or unresponsive to others while "waiting for enlightenment" is a severe abuse of contemplative practice. We may sense that clear vision is the only means of achieving true morality. And we can hope and trust that our practice will indeed help our vision become clearer. But in the process we are bound to respect the senses of duty, responsibility and caring which are our heritage.

In practice, then, our sense is to exercise the fullest, most clear sense of social responsiveness which our vision allows us to perceive at present, and to be working continually in the direction of clearing that vision. We try to encourage this in our groups in two ways. First, a very large number of our contemplative exercises are focused on compassion. This tends to balance other, more self-exploratory experiences. Secondly, we ask questions. In our group discussions we try to foster repeated evaluations of self-interest vs. concern for others. Again and again we raise the issues of compassion, love and service, asking participants to examine their attitudes and behavior forthrightly and to relate their experience to their tradition. We seek to avoid the imposition of arbitrary values in this questioning, while at the same time not allowing the questions to be avoided. In essence this approach is similar to that used in exploring psychological issues and questions of faith which arise during the course of contemplative practice. Here again the responsibility falls upon the group leader to help participants press on into clearer and more honest exploration of their thoughts, sensations and behavior.

As an example, the following discussion might take place after the silence in a typical group:

Leader:	Does anyone have something they'd like to share?
Participant:	I had a lot of trouble getting quiet today. I don't know why. It just seemed as if there was too much going on in my mind. But one thing that did happen was that I began to see a series of faces. Some of them were people I know—family, friends, people I'd met a long time ago. And then there were lots of other faces, strange ones, from all over the world. People who were hungry, or hurting, you know, people who were suffering. I don't know what that means, but it was kind of powerful. I guess I felt like we were all related, or part of the same kind of thing. I'm not sure.
Another Participant:	That's happened to me several times too. It's like a sense of all being together, but there's something disquieting about it. There's so much pain in the world . . .so much suffering.
Leader:	Where does that sense come from . . . that feeling of so much suffering?
First Participant:	Well, I think I felt I should be helping them somehow, like there was this one group of people, people right around me who had all the food they needed—even more than they needed, and all these luxuries, and then there were all these others who didn't have anything. Maybe it's like a sense of injustice, and wondering why?
Leader:	Any sense of "you" in all of that? Your relation to it?
First Participant:	Not really while it was happening, but now afterwards, there's something like guilt, or I wish I could so something.
Second Participant:	It makes me sad, there's something impotent about it. How can you ever really do anything to ease that suffering, really?
Leader:	Maybe it's deeply sensing that it's all there—having your eyes open to it. Me, if I see a problem I can't do anything about, I usually just shut it out. It's hard to go ahead and see what's there even though you feel you can't do anything

about it. Maybe that has something to do with compassion—seeing how it is very clearly, and if you can't do anything then maybe you feel some of that other person's pain and frustration because they can't do anything about it either?

Second
Participant: That does hurt. A lot.

First
Participant: Yes, but it's a clean kind of pain. I mean, it feels like you're really seeing what's there.

Leader: What's the relationship between that clean pain and compassion? No, it seems like that clean pain is part *of* compassion. Does that have anything to do with guilt?

First
Participant: Well it's like you want to help, not, not because you should, but just because somebody needs something—that's not guilt, is it?

Another
Participant: No, guilt is when you're deciding not to do something you know you should do. This is different. It's like feeling someone else's pain as if it were your own . . .

Third
Participant: Well maybe it really *is* your own.

Leader: What does it mean to respond then, to do something about it? When *do* you respond, and how?

In this example, the leader is really doing two things. First, she is sharing some of her own questions, ideas and experiences. Secondly, she's asking questions which will help press the group into deeper clarification of their own perceptions.

Another time when it is very appropriate to question the area of responsiveness to others is when an individual begins to evaluate changes which are occurring within himself or herself. An example:

Participant: Over the past few weeks, since I've been meditating more regularly, it just seems that things go easier. I'm not so uptight about things. All my work gets done, but it's like it doesn't take so much effort.

Leader: What about your relationships with other people?

Participant: Well, they don't hassle me so much. I used to try to meet everybody's demands. You know, do what they wanted me to do rather than what I want to do. Now I just don't get so hooked by that kind of stuff.

Leader: .   Yes, that's one side of it. how you respond to others' demands and expectations. The other side is how you respond to what other people *need*—you know, their pain or their suffering. What's it like with that?

Here the participant is describing something which is very commonly experienced; a feeling of increasing freedom from the demands and expectations of others. This is a rather "psychological" freeing, which has its roots in the degree to which an individual has to rely on satisfying others in order to feel good about himself or herself. At this point the leader could have chosen to explore that dimension more fully by asking "What about the demands and expectations you place on *yourself*?" This would be a good question, but it does delve deeper into personal psychology. In this case, the leader chose to raise a more other-oriented question; to press towards examining how this freeing actually helps a person become *more responsive to* others, if indeed it does. Both directions are valid and worthy of exploration. The important thing is that within the overall tenor of the group, a balance be kept between self-interest and other interest.

All of the discussion concerning proper behavior and social responsiveness has been based on the fact that people *feel* separate from one another and from God. Some contemplative approaches might suggest that deliberations based on this sense of separateness are a waste of time, and that one's energies had better be spent on realizing the basic oneness of all of us. However, we believe that since we must go on living in the world until that uncertain time of "enlightenment" comes, we have an obligation to live in that world in the best way we can. We see through a glass darkly for a very long time, and thus we cannot make ultimate statements about the values of our actions. But we also feel that our contemplative practice and our prayers to do the will of God lead us to increasingly clearer perceptions and accurate action long before our vision is totally purified. Thus while our end goal may be the realization of union with God, many helpful insights can be gained along the path towards that goal. Perhaps it is these insights, the "fringe benefits" along the way, that will constitute the true richness of contemplative practice for most of us.

There are many times in the course of contemplative practice, and there are many times in each group meeting when the self-other dichotomy seems to be eradicated. Though these are only temporary times, they are very precious, and it is important that they not be overlooked. At times such as these, one would have to pull oneself back into separation in order to talk *about* the experience. Therefore it is often much better, then, to say nothing at all.

To summarize, many basic problems of morality seem to be contingent on our seeing ourselves as separate, operating out of our own ego-centered desires and attachments. One of the goals of contemplative practice is to diminish the intensity of this separateness and ego attachments. The assumption is that as this happens, one will come more fully

into harmony with Divine Will and compassion in mind and action is
more likely to spring forth naturally. But recognizing this as a goal, one
still has to accept the fact that most of the time we do feel separate and
we do operate on the basis of ego attachment. Then it becomes important to acknowledge the value of moral action, of seeing what is as
clearly and purely as possible, and of constant and repeated questioning
of one's actions and perceptions. In this arena one *must* ask whether one
is being selfish or not.

In the last analysis, one is never out of social action. There is no way
one can escape the impact one has upon the world. Even retreating to a
mountain cave has its effects upon one's family, friends and colleagues.
The only question then is how true compassion fits into one's behavior.
The pathways of compassion are extremely varied and complex when
one attempts to view them objectively and from a distance. But within
each individual's personal experience of life, true compassion is too
simple for words. It is not so much a matter of meeting needs, or of doing
what one ought, or of figuring out how to help someone. It is simply the
way one lives when the bonds of self-importance are broken.

7

Man and Woman

Sexuality and Contemplative Practice

Most of Shalem's major interests are those one would expect in any contemplative program; methods of prayer and meditation, relating contemplative experience to faith and daily life, etc. The relationship between sexuality and spirituality however, has occupied a special interest for us. There are several reasons for this. A few early participants had spent some time with Tarthang Tulku in Berkeley, and one of the things they had brought back with them was a Tibetan Tantric form of meditation meant to be done by a man and woman together. Our experience with this exercise were so strong and illuminating that it quickly found its way into our regular curriculum. In so doing, it helped to sensitize us all to the importance of the male-female dyad in spiritual growth.

In addition, many of Shalem's leaders and participants have had occasion to meet William Davidson, a psychiatrist who for several years had been exploring the relationship between maleness and femaleness. His experience and reading had led him to see that male and female were formed as equal, complementary and interdependent aspects of a basic unity, and it was his contention that maleness without femaleness or vice versa is always incomplete and partial. He maintained that only with complete complementarity and harmony between the sexual forces could human creativity be actualized. His ideas resonated with others

81

we had encountered in a variety of places. Some of us had been interested in Jungian psychology and were well aware of its emphasis on the importance of males integrating their feminine aspect (anima) and females their masculine aspect (animus). Others of us had been drawn to an exploration of the ancient Yin-Yang complementarity of opposites which has been such an important symbolism in Taoism and other Eastern religions.

But the most important factor in all of this was the woman's liberation movement. We are all part of a culture which is struggling to repair the wounds of generations of male supremacy and female oppression. Many of our early participants had been deeply sensitized to these issues, and we were all ready to experience something more gentle, something that offered a resolution to sexual conflicts as well as inequality.

From the beginning we shared a sense that true spiritual growth had to lead to some kind of wholeness, which would include some healing, integrating harmony between the sexes. We could also see that in our culture this harmony was not occurring as the result of one sex pushing or pulling against the other. It had to come quietly, mutually, in a way which would be free from attachment or mastery. Our experience with Davidson's ideas, tantric mysticism and sexual symbols led us to feel that sexual wholeness, like psychological wholeness, is an *original, natural state* rather than something to be engineered or attained. The way to its realization then, would be through simplification rather than increased complexity, through relaxation rather than tension.

We discovered support for this idea in a myriad of sources. In Genesis there are striking dyadic implications in the account of God creating male and female "in Our image." In ancient Tibetan Tankhas and Hindu paintings the central dieties regularly combine masculine and feminine components. In many Eastern theologies the supreme dieties have specific masculine and feminine manifestations. All of these communicate that while the essence of the diety lies beyond sexual difference, it comes into fullness only through the complementary expression of these differences.

We also discovered an amazingly rich history of sexual complementarity in Christian mysticism. For example, we learned of a large number of saints whose lives were deeply influenced by a "spiritual friend" of the opposite sex. In 1976 Dolores Leckey produced a paper describing some of these relationships* including Francis of Assisi and Clare,

---

*Dolores Leckey, "Growing in the Spirit: Notes on Spiritual Direction and Sexuality," Alban Institute, Washington, D.C. 1976.

Catherine of Siena and Raymond of Capua, John of the Cross and Teresa of Avila, and others.

Upon my first readings in contemplative Christianity, I was struck by the sexual language and symbolism which the medieval mystics used to describe their spiritual journeys. The soul was often seen as the bride, with Christ or God as the bridegroom. Just as often the Holy Spirit was cast in the role of lover in very erotic terms.

Thus there is a great cultural and historical emphasis on sexuality and spirituality. But the strongest motivation for our exploration came from our own direct experience in contemplative practice.

For example, it is not at all uncommon for erotic feelings to be encountered during individual prayer and meditation. Sometimes these experiences seem wholly sexual in nature, being sexual fantasies similar to those which occur in dreams. Sometimes this kind of imagery is seen by the individual as a distraction or "entertainment" which the mind produces to keep things from becoming quiet. But just as often the experiences take on a more deeply "spiritual" tone. At times during meditative practice, experiences of quiet, beauty, belonging, meaning, and closeness to God may be accompanied by distinctly sexual feelings. Several people have described the most outstanding of their contemplative experiences in terms of sex and love.

"I think I have fallen in love with the Universe," one person said. Another said:

> It's like being in love—real adolescent romantic ecstatic love, but I'm not sure who it is that I'm in love with. It's easy to say I love God, but it's a little upsetting to think of myself as falling in love *with* God.

It is understandable that such strong emotions can be disturbing to the individual. We are all pilgrims in a culture which has gone to extremes in attempting to divorce sexuality from spirituality. Our general cultural assumptions convey that spirit and body are irrevocably separate and conflictual, that sexual energy is detrimental to spiritual growth, and that erotic sensations have no place in religious settings. This assumption seems to be held in spite of the obvious sexualization of many "primitive" religious rituals and the obviously spiritual terms which people use to describe sexual experiences.

Much of the terminology we use to describe spiritual growth can be seen to have sexual overtones. Words such as "union," "wholeness," "fulfillment," "bliss," "ecstasy," and "belonging," combine with symbols of love, endearment, adoration and worship and feelings of joining, longing, hunger and vulnerability to produce an atmosphere which can become highly sexualized. The relationship between sexuality and spirituality is so deep and pervasive that one might wonder why sexuality does not appear even *more* frequently in contemplative practice.

A good deal of theological and psychological energy has been spent trying to deal with this. On the humanistic side of the spectrum, Freud saw all these connections and concluded that religion was a defensive vehicle for the displacement of unacceptable eroticism. On the theological side, there have been many attempts to discriminate between conceptualizations of *eros*, the genital-sexualized or biological love; *philia*, or brotherly love, *agape*, the transcendent love of the Divine for humankind, and numerous other categories. The mystics of both East and West seem more comfortable with images of sexualized love for the Divine, but at the same time they proclaim the ideal of wholeness which comes from transcending all sexual and other subject-object dichotomies. The idea here is that once the individual goes beyond the need to discriminate between subject and object, love and sexual energy lose their specific attachments and exist freely everywhere all the time. Then the body is seen as the material barometer of concentrated or moving energy. At this point, one no longer needs to discriminate between kinds of love. Love is simply the way the universe is. It is synonymous with life.

This sort of intellectual discourse usually arises as an attempt to explain human experience. But ironically it often seems to keep one's mind at a great distance *from* that experience. And it is experience rather than philosophy which propels people into a search for spiritual deepening. Feeling unfulfilled, people sometimes find it difficult to decide whether that lack of fulfillment is sexual-interpersonal or "spiritual" in nature. Similarly, sophisticated individuals sometimes wonder if they might be using contemplative practice as a way of escaping from or coping with sexual feelings. Many people fear that in order to grow in spirit they may have to sacrifice some or all of their sexuality. And always there is the question of how to understand the strong emotions encountered in contemplative practice. Where do they come from? Are they "spiritual" or "sexual?" Are they good or bad, a help or a hindrance?

One of our basic assumptions concerning spirituality and sexuality is identical with that concerning spirituality and psychology; namely that much of the trouble comes from our having separated the two into distinct and opposing entities. As is the case with so much of human struggling, the problem seems to lie in having to relate to dualistic images and conceptions of reality rather than to things-as-they-are. This is true for the dichotomies people draw between male and female. To be sure, there are basic differences between male and female. There are also basic differences between all people, between species of trees and kinds of rocks. But the existence of such differences does not mean that separation and objectification have to take place. It is only in people's thought-concepts that such separations and objectifications occur, and when they do occur, the stage is set for inevitable struggle. As we have said in so many ways before, wholeness, compassion and fulfillment do not come through the resolution of such artificially determined differences. Nor do they come through the establishment of cooperation, or even ultimately through reconciliation. Rather, they come in fullness when one's own mental processes of objectification and separation cease, when one's images of the world fall away and things can be seen just-as-they are. Only then can one cease one's troublesome *thinking about* life and get on with living.

In practice, the cessation of this kind of thinking may occur in surprising settings. For example, we have found that one of the best ways in which the male-female duality can be transcended is through direct and immediate confrontation of a man and a woman. With all the emotional loading and cultural overlay concerning sexuality, one might expect that a male-female dyad would be an unlikely setting for such transcendence to take place. But we have found that just the opposite is true.

Our deepest insights into this phenomenon have come through experience with male-female pairing in spiritual friendships and with the Tibetan tantric exercise. The tantric exercise is a simple and direct way for people to begin to experience some true clarification of the entire male-female-wholeness issue. It has been so revealing to us that it will be described in some detail here. It can be a very powerful experience, and it should not be undertaken lightly. Participants should take part only if they feel comfortable with the idea after having had the exercise described to them. And an opportunity to "process" the experience afterwards in a calm and secure atmosphere is important. We would advise that the exercise not be tried until after people have had some experience with contemplative practice.

In its original Tibetan form, the exercise took many hours to complete and involved very long periods of motionless sitting. For our purposes the exercise has been considerably "Americanized" but it still takes nearly two hours to accomplish. It consists of three periods of silence followed by some time to discuss and process the experience. We have found the following form useful, and would advise against changing or adapting it any more than we already have.

1. A man and woman are paired for the exercise. We usually attempt to pair people who do not already have a significant relationship

with each other. This helps them minimize extraneous feelings and allows them to focus primarily on the personhood of each other. The procedure is explained prior to beginning so that instructions will not need to be given during the course of the exercise. The entire exercise is done in silence.

2. The man and woman seat themselves comfortably, facing each other at a distance of about three feet.

3. For twenty to thirty minutes, they simply watch each other, preferably focusing on each other's eyes. During this time, they are simply open to whatever thoughts or feelings may occur, letting them come and go, not trying to hold any special image or thought. Often at the beginning there is some anxiety and social embarrassment which may be expressed through giggles or fidgiting. Often this happens simply because people are not used to looking at each other without talking. The participants are instructed ahead of time that if this occurs they should not struggle against it, but should just wait it out and see it through. Soon the couple settles down and can look at each other quite openly, in the same way they might watch a candle while meditating.

4. At the end of this period (the time is kept by the leader or someone not participating in the exercise) the couple takes a silent break for five minutes. During this time they may stretch, lie down, lean back or move about, but should not leave the room.

5. After the break the couple resumes the seated positions. During the next twenty to thirty minutes they look at each other and try, in their own minds, to "exchange" themselves with the other person; to "become" the other person and allow the other to "become" oneself. They may do this in any way they wish, but again they should remain open and allow thoughts and feelings to come and go freely. It is best not to give the participants any specific instructions as to *how* to go about trying to become the other.

6. After this, another five-minute break.

7. The final ten minutes are really just relaxation and individual open meditation. The man and woman do not need to look at each other, and are just simply open to whatever thoughts or feelings may come to them during this time.

8. After the final period, the two can discuss their experiences. They may do this alone first and then in small groups.

9. After some initial discussion, it is important that the participants discuss the experience with the leader present. Usually this is done in a group setting.

People have a variety of experiences during this exercise, but the most common and striking feature with our participants has been an awareness of "energy." Perceptions of this energy have led us to what we feel are very basic and important insights into the spiritual significance of maleness and femaleness, and have brought us fresh ways of perceiving the nature of love and sexuality. A typical account of the experience as described by a woman might be as follows:

> When we first sat down I was a little nervous. We both were. We smiled a little, but pretty soon it all quieted down. During the first twenty minutes I guess I just sort of explored his face. Kind of getting to know him that way. Then I got off on a whole lot of side-trips, memories and images of other people, distractions here and there. At first there was a real sense of us being two people having to relate to each other, but very soon that went away, and—it seems strange looking back—but it was like he was just there, nothing special about it. He could have been a table or a chair. Then I sort of came back to him as a person, and that time maybe there was a little awareness of our sexual difference, but nothing strong. I do remember feeling some affectionate, sort of warm feelings towards him, like I'd like to know him better. Somewhere along there I almost began to cry. I don't know why. But it passed quickly. Then for a while his face seemed to change a lot. Maybe my eyes were getting tired from looking at him. At first I tried to keep him in focus, but then I realized that was holding on, so I just let my gaze become blurry, and his face really changed a lot. Some of the changes were interesting, and some were a little scary. It seemed that at one time his face would look very old, then very young, then like someone else entirely. Then, towards the end, I felt very calm, and it seemed like something was very vibrant or energetic down deep—but very quiet.
>
> The second twenty minutes was hard for me, especially at the beginning. I didn't know how to "become" him. I tried thinking about what he might be feeling or thinking. I wished I knew him better so I could identify with him more. I couldn't really get into "becoming" him, but about halfway through I sort of gave up and then I began to feel like we really were together. Like sometimes our eyes would blink at the same time, or we'd move slightly together—the closeness was incredible. There was something really powerful going on, almost scary at times. The time was over before I knew it. Nothing special happened during the third twenty minutes. I just relaxed and felt . . . sort of calm and alert. I really enjoyed talking afterwards. I've never in my life really looked at another person that way.

When people discuss their experiences in depth, the following sequence often emerges: The first feeling of energy is vague, undefined, down deep, seeming to generate some restlessness, anxiety and thinking. Then the energy goes through a surprisingly short phase of sexualization. This usually happens early in the second period and may be associated with feelings of affection, empathy, desire for closeness, or actual sexual attraction. Then, rather rapidly, the energy seems to leave the sexual or me-you dimension and becomes much more powerful, taking on a transcendent quality which people find difficult to describe. At this point there often seems to be a very deep combining or unity of experience which leaves feelings of attraction or repulsion far behind.

The recognition of this energy and the changes it goes through may reveal some important insights into daily experiences of sexuality, love, and male-female consciousness. It is as if the entire spectrum of love, from *eros* to *agapé,* is comprised of the same basic energy. In fact, this appears to be the same common energy which forms other feelings, such as fear, aspiration, anger or longing. The precise *form* which the energy takes seems to be determined by the images and preconceptions with which people characteristically view certain situations. For example, when a man and woman meet and some intrapsychic energy becomes activated, they *expect* their feelings to be sexual, fearful, curious, etc., and therefore the energy seems to take that form. But if they ease their hold on their expectations by allowing the feelings to come and go freely, the energy seems to move on to less objectified levels. According to this theory, it is not the energy itself which changes, but rather the individual's openness to and perception of that energy.

Similarly, if one is insulted by another person, energy is released which is usually identified as anger because anger is what is expected. In this case too, if the "anger" is held lightly and allowed to be free, one can see it seeming to change into a less-differentiated form of energy which may have an almost unlimited number of possibilities for expression.

This way of understanding the energy of human emotions is very similar to that found in some Eastern religious-psychologies, and is in keeping with much of the tradition of tantric yoga. It has numerous ramifications for both psychology and theology, but for us it has been most illuminating in the area of sexuality and spirituality. It appears that the male-female combination is one in which considerable amounts of this basic energy are released, and this seems to account for the greatly enhanced creativity we have seen in male-female teamwork and spiritual friendships. It does not seem that the triggering of this energy is simply a result of genital-sexual displacement as might be postulated by Freudian psychology, for it happens in marriage relationships where there are no sexual prohibitions as well as in celibate relationships such as those of our spiritual friends. What does seem to happen is that through the complementarity of maleness and femaleness, a kind of "channel" opens through which energy can be expressed in greatly increased creativity and efficiency.

It is for this reason that insofar as possible we attempt to pair men and women in our spiritual friendships, keep a balanced number of women and men in our groups, and use male/female teams for group leadership.

The ramifications and implications of the sexual dyad are immense, and have only barely been addressed here. But most importantly for the purposes of contemplative spiritual practice, we have come to feel that sexual feelings and consciousness of sexuality are not only normal parts of spiritual growth, but also that far from being obstacles to that growth they are signals of a release of energy and an intuitive acknowledgement of the basic unity of all things.

Sexuality only becomes an obstacle when for one reason or another it is held too tightly or pushed away too forcefully so that its underlying energy is not free. Almost inevitably this happens when one begins to see another person as an object and develops feelings of possessiveness or desire for personal ego-gratification through that other person. Here behavioral boundaries, though necessary, are insufficient. Again, the problem boils down to self-importance and narrowness of vision. The course of contemplative practice is to allow this self-importance to diminish and vision to expand. This happens, as one is able to ease one's grips on personal desires and preconceptions, and in the process one moves into increasing harmony with the most basic forces and energies of life.

As this happens, one begins to see that there can be no true conflict between man and woman since they are essential parts of a larger whole. Neither one nor the other, but the *two* are made in the image of God. It becomes clear that for the sexes to fight, or to try to possess, restrict or conquer each other is like the hand attacking its arm. Only injury and suffering can result.

Similarly, the distinctions between eros, philia, agapé and other "forms" of love can be seen simply as differing ways in which we conceptualize and respond to basic life-energy. The most sublime forms of love, the pure compassion of Buddhism, the devotional Bhakti of Hinduism, the agapé of Christianity, are manifestations of that energy in its least-fettered form.

When one's images, preconceptions and prejudices about love are allowed to fall away, things can be seen just as they are. And when one's attachments to possessiveness, envy and jealousy are allowed to relax, things can be allowed to *be* just as they are. And finally, when things can both be seen and allowed to be just as they are, nothing but the Divine love remains.

8

Many Paths Or One?

Ecumenical Spiritual Practice

As has been discussed previously, one of the most enduring characteristics of Shalem has been the exploration of different religious approaches to spirituality as a means of enriching the appreciation of one's
own religious heritage. By its very nature this process fosters a growing
ecumenical consciousness. Of course there never was any real doubt
that Shalem would be an ecumenical undertaking, given its interfaith
base in METC. The question was simply what form that ecumenism
would take.

Shalem's early leadership already recognized some of the deep
similarities between world religions and many of us suspected that, at
least on an experiential as opposed to a symbolic/interpretive level, the
contemplative and esoteric core of these religions could be seen as
basically the same.* As an example, one can look at certain transcendent or mystical experiences and see that they have common features
regardless of the specific religious context in which they occur. If one
takes a rather secular and psychological look at a certain category of
"peak" religious experiences, they consistently seem to share at least
three factors. Whether the experience is labeled as conversion or cosmic

---

*Tilden H. Edwards, "Criss-crossing the Christian-Buddhist Bridge," p. 185, from
REFLECTIONS OF MIND, Dharma Publishing, California, 1975.

consciousness, satori or transcendence, these three factors always seem to be present. The first of these factors can be called *awareness*. It includes a sense of expanded or heightened consciousness of one's surroundings—a subjective feeling of increased acuity and complete-ness of perception. Usually this is accompanied by present-centeredness of attention and a sense of letting go or relaxation into life as-it-is. It is often associated with a feeling of deep peace and calm.

Second there is a sense of *unity* with life in which, at least for the duration of the immediate experience, self-definition and self-interest cease to be of importance. This may be described as surrender, giving over to the Divine Will, merging with the universe, or being at one with God, with Christ or with the cosmos. In lesser degrees this phenomenon manifests itself as a feeling of belonging, being accepted, or being loved by the ultimate power of the universe. In greater degrees, it approaches the point of complete union.

Finally, such experiences include what might be called a *reactive* element; the individual's response *to* the experience. This is charac-terized by feelings of awe, wonder, and a curious mixture of fear and bliss. It is also in this reactive component that sensations of ineffability, fulfillment, and certitude occur.

There has been a good deal of psychological and theological study of such experiences, and it has long been known that they are not the exclusive property of any one religion. In fact, it has been shown that such experiences occur frequently outside the context of organized religions. They happen spontaneously from time to time in the lives of nearly all human beings. It has been suggested that the "religiousness" of these experiences is simply that they raise such deep feelings and questions about the meaning of one's existence that they force one into religious considerations. Thus it may be *after the fact* of these experi-ences that many differing religious explanations are derived, each as a means of attempting to understand and integrate the experiences. And it may be in these explanations, in the *thinking about* the experiences, that differing theological stances occur. There are of course many other kinds of religious experiences. But even in the varying visionary and prophetic experiences recounted in the world's religions, one can see many similarities. Moses, Mohammed, Jesus, Buddha, and a host of others experienced shaking revelations after periods of retreat and purification. Needless to say, there is much more to religion than simple attempts to explain transcendent experiences. Still it is continually striking that so many experiences, at core, seem to be similar in every major religious tradition.

In this light, it made even more sense for Shalem to explore the possibilities of a truly ecumenical approach to spiritual growth. Being sponsored by the Metropolitan Ecumenical Training Center, Shalem had an ideal opportunity for this. METC had experienced considerable success in ecumenical approaches to social justice issues and theological education, and it seemed reasonable to hope that similar success would occur in spiritual formation. The problem was to explore the degrees and the ways in which differing traditions could come together in the search for spiritual growth. Out of our work in this area has come a very valuable clarification of our openness and limitations in terms of crossing denominational and world religion boundaries.

One of these limitations is that people who are already deeply committed to a certain religious tradition or community need to explore their deepest spiritual perceptions *within the context* of that tradition or community wherever that is possible. An ecumenical approach which attempts to cover all traditions is often too bland, superficial, or scattered for those with a strong sense of pre-existing community. For example, there is often ample opportunity within Black American churches for outward expression of deep spiritual searching and experience. There seems less need, then, for many black people to find any "special" or extracommunal vehicle in order to meet this need.

Sometimes even if a tradition offers little in the way of norms for communal expression of the personal spiritual quest, commitment to the tradition may be so strong that an ecumenical approach is not acceptable. In the Jewish tradition, for example, there seems to be no recent norm for the spiritual quest *separate from* the communal prayer experience. Many Jews would find it problematical as to whether non-communal spiritual practice could be seen as a validly Jewish enterprise. To engage in a contemplative group outside one's tradition might be seen as a compromise of religious authenticity for many Christians as well as Jews.

Another limitation has been our increasingly heavy emphasis on *contemplative* spirituality. In the beginning, we had hardly even seen this as an emphasis. We felt very open to spiritual paths which rely more upon action or devotion rather than silent prayer and meditation, and we felt there was no conflict between such approaches. We continue to *feel* this way, but in practice, in our long-term groups, the emphasis on contemplative prayer and meditation has continually gained prominence. This emphasis reflects the evolving preferences of the majority of our leaders and participants as well as a sense of the relative unavailability of help on a Western contemplative way compared to other paths.

Thus, whether we wanted it to or not, some beginning sense of standardization, perhaps even orthodoxy, has begun to emerge, and this of course limits the degree to which we can be fully responsive to all other approaches. In general, Shalem participants and leaders seem to have developed a sense that social responsiveness and devotion to God need to grow out of the experience of silence; that one's individual prayer life needs to be the ground from which one's actions spring.

This immediately raises ecumenical questions, for there are many religious orientations in this country which place these factors in an almost reverse order, indicating that one's good works and devotion are what determine the depth and quality of one's personal spiritual silence. We find no rational theological quarrel with this, and in fact many of us have come to feel that *any* priority arrangement of silence-versus-action is problematical. But in practice, it seems that most of our leaders and participants have been drawn to an emphasis on contemplative practice in the long-term groups, and not everyone can be comfortable with this form of spiritual practice and expression. Specifically, while we have found most responsiveness with Roman Catholics and Episcopalians with this approach (both of which have contemplation built into their heritage), it seems less amenable to traditional Black and Jewish orientations. "Mainline" Protestant orientations generally fall somewhere in between these two groups.

In much of the black religious community, for example, it would be thought that to sit for extended periods of time in silence is a bit of a luxury. Even to come to a weekly group meeting where the emphasis is on contemplative practice would often seem somehow out of order when there is so much work needing to be done. And since many black American churches have preserved a greater integration of spirituality within their ongoing activities of worship and service than have many mainline white churches, there may be less felt need for *additional experiential* dimensions.

In our examination of these differences, it seems that the "something else," the "something spiritual" for which so many people hunger often boils down to what could be called *an emotional investment in faith*. This is faith at a feeling level, a gut-certainty which undergirds rational theological belief. Some of our black leaders and participants have helped the rest of us to see that many black congregations provide this kind of nourishment far more deeply and consistently than the so-called mainline white churches have.

Many pentecostal, charismatic and evangelical traditions, both black and white, actively provide such emotional and experiential nourishment to their members. People of such orientations might easily feel that there simply is "not enough happening" in more contemplative approaches like Shalem's. Their assumption would be that it is better to spend one's time and energy *actively* praying, worshipping, praising and doing the works of God in the context of their own community of faith.

Thus, within the Christian community there are many sectors which do not experience such a felt need for contemplative spirituality as do the so-called mainline churches. And even when there *is* a felt need for deeper spiritual growth, an ecumenical contemplative approach focused on intuitive rather than affective awareness may not be the answer.

The Christian-Jewish spiritual relationship has been a rich field of discovery for us in this regard. While Judaism includes a deep and ancient tradition of mysticism, there are many areas of difference between Christian and Jewish spirituality which seem to necessitate basic differences in contemplative practice. In Christian spirituality, for example, "grace" and "The Holy Spirit" are commonly referred to and in fact *felt* as playing an integral role in one's life and growth. There is little in the usual Jewish tradition which can correlate with these concepts. Instead, there is a deeply felt consciousness of history, heritage and belonging to each other and to God which could never be fully duplicated in a Christian context.

As another example, prayer tends to mean different things to Christians and Jews. While Christians readily use prayer as a tool for the accomplishment of certain ends, for many Jews prayer has more the quality of a command—an end-in-itself that is required by Covenant. While most Christians see spiritual development as something "added to" life to deepen and enrich it, for many Jews spirituality is such an integral part *of* life that it cannot even be seen as a distinct aspect of experience. In this sense, the Jewish experience is not unlike that of native American Indian religions* where spirituality and peoplehood are inextricably intertwined.

Thus, while there are many similarities between the Jewish and Christian faiths, there are also some basic differences which strike quite close to the heart of contemplative practice. Christians and Jews have little difficulty working together in many areas, and can often even begin to work on their spiritual growth within a common context. But as this spiritual "work" proceeds, there comes a time when the experience and practice must be integrated in terms of faith and peoplehood and at this point the paths must diverge again.

This point is a critical one, and it is both wonderful and painful. It is wonderful because it is the point at which Christians tend to become more Christian and Jews become more Jewish. It is the point at which

*Cf. Chapter 10, "Voices of Authority: Interviews with Twenty-Nine Spiritual Leaders and Groups."

people begin to recognize previously undiscovered richness in their own religious roots. But it is painful because these roots are indeed different, and they require different kinds of nourishment. They are different "ways in" to the Holy One, and they need to occur within the context of their specific communities.

At the point of this relating of experience to community, the true richness of our many-faceted human family can be seen. As human beings, we share common experiences, similar hungers for truth, commonalities of searching for God. We can celebrate and share these signs of our unity, across all racial and cultural lines. And, hopefully, we can nurture and enrich each other's growth. But as must be learned repeatedly in all areas of life, this recognition of "togetherness" cannot be pushed into a contrived image of "sameness." Each of us needs his or her own roots, his or her own community and heritage within the family of humanity. This means that these are levels of spirituality which can only be fulfilled within the context of one's community.

This recognition applies to all traditions and communities, but for Shalem it has been most visibly affirmed by our experience with modern Jewish and Black Christian traditions. Finding that our typical contemplative groups attracted few Blacks and Jews, Shalem decided to offer one group specifically for Blacks and another specifically for Jews.

The Jewish group, called "The Aleph Gate," focused on specifically Jewish spiritual practice including candle meditations, scriptural work and story telling. It was small in size, short in length, but seen as helpful by many of its participants. Several Christians joined the group, which was discomforting to some of the Jewish members because of its diffusion of the group's Jewish authenticity. The Black group drew so few members that it was cancelled. Thus Shalem's offerings continued to be directed primarily towards "mainline" Christians. This seems to reflect where the need lies for "ecumenical" contemplative groups. It seems likely that most Jews will need to explore their spiritual hunger within a Jewish context from the outset unless they are so alienated from their tradition that they need to make considerably more distant pilgrimages. It seems that the same is true for those Black Americans who identify with the distinctive evangelical faith of their forebears.

Each religious group has the opportunity of making whatever pilgrimage is necessary within the context of its own history and community. No doubt these pilgrimages will involve the meeting of other traditions and communities. And if they are true pilgrimages, they will all lead not only towards an enrichment of their own traditions, but towards open compassion for all other human beings. They will all lead towards that deepest sense of organic relatedness with humanity, and even beyond that, towards the One. They will all be pilgrimages home.

In summary then, we have come to feel that at its core, spiritual growth *does* transcend denominational, ethnic and personal boundaries, just as do basic transcendental experiences. Further, all legitimate spiritual approaches seem to include a balance of action and contemplation, devotion and works. But the *ways* in which one goes about intentionally seeking to enhance one's spiritual growth may need to differ according to one's religious and cultural orientation as well as one's personality and point in life. Even more importantly, the *community context* with which this takes place will need to be as authentic as possible.

It is better for an ecumenical organization to offer different paths or tracks for spiritual development geared to the needs of people of differing orientations rather than attempt to mix everyone together in an undifferentiated amalgamation. In addition, the leadership of those groups should share the orientation and background of the participants. Then, while members of a given group may taste the attitudes and approaches of differing traditions, they will be doing so together, in the context of their own tradition.

There are, of course, many people in our society who are unaware of their own tradition, or who are engaged in some form of rebellion against it. These individuals may need some time to explore differing tracks in the process of uncovering their own true roots.

To be viable, every religion needs openness to God's truth no matter how it may be manifested, but we have felt from the outset and believe even more fervently now that the utmost respect must be given to the specific religious tradition from which each individual comes. To blur the distinctions between these traditions in the name of ecumenism or commonality is a very dangerous practice. Too much avoidance of tradition can lead to psychologizing and secularizing one's attitudes toward spiritual growth. This in turn increases the likelihood of seeing spiritual growth as a *thing* to be acquired in addition to and divorced from the full richness and communal accountability of one's religious heritage. Such an attitude can only serve to alienate us further from our nature and from God.

Part III
Practice

9

Getting Started

Suggestions for the Establishment and Conduct of Groups

Having discussed our experiences with contemplative spiritual development groups, we can now make some specific suggestions as to how one may go about beginning such a group. Usually the group will be organized within a pre-existing institution. Perhaps it is a congregation in which a few people have expressed the desire to deepen their experience of prayer. Or maybe during the course of worship planning or adult education a need for corporate spiritual practice emerges. Perhaps the setting is a religious community, theological school or clinical training program in which certain people have identified a need for a more coherent look at contemplative practice. Or it could be a religiously oriented training and consultation program which wishes to respond to the spiritual needs of its constituents.

To date, about the only option for a person who feels a need for contemplative experience has been to leave his or her primary community (congregation, school, etc.) and go elsewhere to participate in an established training program which represents some specific spiritual tradition. This is a lonely undertaking and it often forces the individual to withdraw at least some of his or her investment in the primary community. How much more simple, efficient and gentle it would be if that person could embark on a course of spiritual deepening right there *within*

101

his or her basic community. The possibility of this is the hope and the vision we wish to share with you.

If people could develop contemplative groups within their pre-existing communities, the true meaning of "Pilgrimage Home" would be exemplified. And a good deal of unnecessary drama and energy would be saved. The specific needs and desires of the people involved will determine the ultimate structure of any such group, but the suggestions which follow can constitute a model which should be helpful in planning.

The Clarification Process

Whatever the situation, it is important to go through some process of clarifying what is needed before one jumps in to establish a program. It is not possible to plan a program for the exploration of contemplative spirituality without involving those who will be making use of such a program. People need to sense their own personal motivations; it does not suffice for someone else to say, "This is what I think you need so what you should do is . . ."

A good way to begin is to gather together a number of interested people and spend some time exploring what their needs seem to be. Then a program to respond to those needs can be developed. In a congregation for example, the interested people might meet several times in open discussion to explore their sense of need for spiritual deepening. After this they would do well to spend a day or two together working with the Self-Search Format (See Chapter 13). Only after this should they begin to plan any structure for long-term involvement together. A similar procedure can occur with representative members of faculty and students in a training situation.

The importance of this preliminary clarification cannot be over emphasized. While people may find it relatively easy to express a need for "something spiritual" in their lives, things immediately become more difficult when one tries to identify precisely what is meant by those words. During the clarification process it may emerge that what is needed is scripture study, or some program to enrich interpersonal relations, or some re-energizing of corporate worship. The exercises and suggestions given in Chapter 13 will help to make this clear. If such does turn out to be the case, much time and energy can be saved, and the group will not need to dash off to explore various forms of meditation and contemplative prayer. If on the other hand it becomes obvious that some experience with contemplative practice is in order, the group can then proceed to use the material in this book to assist in further planning.

Planning

At the end of the clarification process one cannot expect to have decided upon a hard and fast program. There will still be many unanswered questions, many areas of confusion and vagueness. What will emerge is a sense of immediate direction which should be seen as a "next step" rather than a final course of action. In this sense the establishment of a group for contemplative practice is really another phase of clarification. In fact contemplative practice really is nothing but an ongoing, ever deepening process of clarification. Its intent, at least as we see it, is to keep clearing the obstructions, confusions and prejudices from one's vision. If a contemplative approach is chosen as the way to spiritual deepening, the clarification process will never end.

If the formation of a group for contemplative practice does seem to be in order, we suggest that the planners establish a time-frame of from three to nine months, at which point another major evaluation should take place. In programs lasting less than three months there is not enough time to make a good judgment about the nature of contemplative practice or the effects of that practice on people's lives. For the same reason it is best if the group can plan to meet regularly and consistently during this initial period.

Commitment

Members at this point do need to make a commitment to attending meetings regularly and to practicing as diligently as possible on their own in between the meetings.

The nature of the members' commitment to the group and to practice is a rather delicate one. While it is very important that each person try to stick to a schedule of personal contemplative discipline (mainly consisting of daily silent prayer or meditation and possibly journal keeping) it is also important that the discipline not constitute an obstacle in and of itself. Everyone experiences times when it is difficult, even impossible to sit still. Sometimes these periods last for minutes or hours. At other times they may last for months. If one feels one's commitment is to sit in silence for a certain time every day, and one finds it simply impossible to do so, then guilt and feelings of failure are unnecessarily added to one's practice. Further, many people's minds will rebel against a too-rigid practice commitment, adding even more needless emotional struggle. As a result, contemplative practice can turn out to be more of a burden than a process of relaxing and communion. In any case, the practice is likely to create more confusion than clarity if the commitment is made too rigidly.

It may be best not to ask for a rigid commitment to a specific time or form of practice, but rather to ask that members try to *remember* their practice each day. In this way they will minimize forgetfulness but at the same time they need not feel guilty or ashamed if their practice becomes difficult. The problems and feelings surrounding commitment and discipline are very good material for discussion within the group, and members should be encouraged to share such experiences.

Scheduling

As mentioned above, an overall time frame of from three to nine months is recommended for a beginning exploratory group. Weekly meetings are advised. If meetings are not held this frequently, motivation for practice begins to drop off and experiences cannot be freshly shared. We have found that 1½ hours is an absolute minimum of time required for each meeting. 2 or 2½ hours would be much better. It is very important that the group be able to maintain a relaxed, flowing atmosphere. Therefore it is necessary to insure that meetings are long enough so that the group will not feel pressured to accomplish more than it has time for.

Even if two-hour weekly meetings are scheduled there are frequently times when longer sessions are necessary. Such times occur when there is a need for more extensive evaluation, meetings with spiritual friends, or the presentation of longer contemplative exercises. We have found it helpful to schedule one "long session" each month to take care of this need. For example if a group generally meets for two hours every Thursday evening, it could plan to have a four-hour meeting the first Thursday of each month. This arrangement is especially helpful for beginning groups, because a new contemplative approach can be presented during the long session and then practiced and explored more deeply during the remaining three meetings in the month.

It is unwise to schedule meetings immediately after meals because full stomachs create too much drowsiness in the still atmosphere of contemplative practice. If it is necessary for the group to meet after meal time, members should be advised to eat very lightly or to wait until after the group to eat.

If feasible, it is also good to schedule several day-long sessions or a weekend retreat during the course of the group. Such extended periods of time together are very helpful from several aspects. First, they allow for the presentation of prolonged meditative experiences such as the dyadic or mirror exercises (discussed in Chapter 14). They also permit the group to practice mindfulness together in the more usual daily activities of eating, talking, going to sleep, etc. In addition, the fellowship and support experienced during a day or weekend retreat can seldom be duplicated on the basis of weekly meetings. A time away together such as this is also an ideal opportunity to invite an outside authority or spiritual leader to share his or her thoughts with the group.

Guidelines for Members

At the outset it is wise to establish a few standards for the group. This will avoid wasting precious time later on. Some of these guidelines will involve aspects of commitment to attendance and to practice as previously discussed. Though each group will probably need standards which are particular to it, we have found the following quite helpful:

A. Insofar as possible, members should try to be on time for the meetings. Late arrivals should be kept to a minimum as they can be quite distracting.

B. Socializing and small talk should be limited to before and after the group meetings, and preferably should take place in another room so as not to disturb those who wish to begin early or remain after the group. Many of our group participants have indicated that socializing with other group members before or after the meetings has been a very pleasant and important part of their experience. For some it seems to provide a more secure and relaxed sense of "belonging" in the group. This should not be rigidly discouraged, but neither should it invade the time or space of the meeting.

C. Eating, drinking and smoking are also best reserved for before or after the meeting, and outside the meeting room.

D. Leaving the room during the meeting time should be kept to a minimum.

E. Depending on the setting, some additional guidelines may be helpful regarding members' helping to set up the room before the meeting or picking up afterwards.

F. It is probably best to ask participants to avoid indiscriminate sharing of their experiences with others outside the group. This helps to avoid dissipation of developing experiences and prideful proclamations such as "Look at my great experience!" This is rather tricky, because it is also important not to encourage the reverse kind of pride, "My experience is too profound for you to understand . . . I must keep it secret." In general the attitude here should be "nothing special," nothing worth advertising publicly, nothing worth hoarding privately.

In addition to these "behavioral" standards, it is often helpful to try to establish some ground rules for attitudes and intent. These kinds of guidelines cannot be legislated or in any way enforced, but they can be encouraged. They have to be quite flexible and geared to the specific needs of each group, but we have found the following worthwhile:

Openness

Members can be asked to minimize their expectations and pre-judging of experiences, thus encouraging a conscious openness and receptivity to new approaches. This can help people avoid the mentality of expecting great results and the off-handed rejection of an experience if such expectations are not immediately met. It encourages an attitude of simplicity, of being open and seeing what comes. It also helps overcome certain prejudices and fears regarding approaches which may seem strange or threatening in some way. Finally, it encourages people to explore each approach in depth before making judgments about it.

Acceptance

Participants would do well to nurture a non-judgmental attitude towards the experiences of others. If members can be encouraged to listen carefully to others without immediately trying to jump in and "help" them with advice or correction, then everyone will feel more comfortable in sharing their experiences openly and frankly. This is a vital element in religiously oriented contemplative groups, because people are often fearful of judgment, or of being "preached to" by others. It takes some time for trust to grow in this area, but guidelines such as this can be helpful in speeding up the process.

Being Gentle

Encouraging an attitude of gentleness towards oneself as well as others will help group members be more relaxed and open. It will also minimize people's habitual tendencies to be harsh on themselves in terms of success and failure. One of the hardest preconceptions to overcome is that contemplative practice is like athletic practice with all its emphasis on discipline and effort. In fact, it is often only when ideas of progress and success are given up that true growth seems to occur. This forces one to walk the nebulous line between rigid discipline and laziness. This line, it seems, can never be drawn arbitrarily. An attitude of gentleness can help each person move through the variety of seemingly contradictory experiences which occur along this line.

Lightness

Similarly, it is helpful to encourage an attitude of taking one's spiritual experiences lightly. Because such experiences seem so meaningful and are so loaded with emotions such as longing, fear, joy and hope, it is very easy to become dramatic about them. Once one becomes hooked by this drama, the entire process can take on an almost morbid importance and heaviness. This is a sign of excessive attachment and it breeds a host of difficulties. Success and failure take on increasing significance, and one becomes impatient with other people and other interests. All of this serves to breed a growing sense of self-importance which truly subverts the course of spiritual practice. The best remedy for this sticky importance is an attitude of responding to things lightly, of not taking oneself seriously, of seeing the humor in one's experiences. Again, a fine line has to be explored. There is a polarity between heavy self-importance on the one hand and lack of caring on the other. Lightness and humor can help one to transcend this polarity.

Keeping the Goal in Mind

It is important that in some way the group minimize any tendency to turn itself into a therapy group. Extensive discussion of emotions and interpersonal feelings can waste precious time and encourage self-importance. It should be understood by the members that the intent of the group is to grow in spiritual awareness through contemplative practice rather than to solve psychological problems. Of course there is much vagueness and overlap here and as discussed in Chapter 5 it is not accurate to make too firm a distinction between "psychological" and "spiritual." On the other hand some statement to this effect can be helpful for members in understanding the hazards of becoming sidetracked into an exclusively psychological mentality. To support this approach, it is better to discuss emotions in terms of where they seem to come from in consciousness and how they influence attention and awareness than in terms of their psychodynamic origins or of what to do about them.

Concern for Others

In an attempt to avoid the possibility of excessive self-interest in contemplative practice, there can be a concerted and continuous effort on everyone's part to remain sensitive to the daily struggles and suffering of others in the world. This involves not only reminding oneself of compassionate concerns and actions, but a continuing frank appraisal of the degree and manner in which one is going about responding to these issues in one's daily life. Encouragement of daily intercessory prayer as well as concern and action for others can help make a bridge between solitude and togetherness.

Guidelines such as these can be very helpful in establishing and maintaining a proper atmosphere for the group. But it is the attitude of the group leaders which will be most important. Regardless of the stated standards for the group, if the leaders cannot model these standards, they will be quite meaningless. Therefore it is essential that group leaders feel comfortable with and committed to any such guidelines.

Environment and Material

In most cases the group's meeting place will be dictated by the space available, and sometimes there is little choice about this. If there is some flexibility however, the following considerations may be helpful:

It is best to have a room which will be quiet and relatively free from external distractions. While contemplative practice is extremely difficult when there is a lot of external noise, there is no need to insure *absolute* quiet. Some noise is actually beneficial in helping people learn how to be open to distractions without being disturbed by them. Windows which can be opened to the outside are very helpful, as is carpeting and a comfortable temperature. In good weather, the group may wish to try meeting outside.

There should be sufficient floor space for all group members to engage simultaneously in physical exercise and movement. We encourage our participants to sit on the floor unless some physical problem makes this difficult. There seems to be a greater sense of group commonality if most of the members share the same body position during the silence. More importantly, it is easier for many people to maintain a physical posture of relaxed alertness if one is sitting on the floor than if one is on a chair. Consequently, there is less likelihood of sleepiness or dulled awareness. We ask each of our participants to bring a cushion or rolled-up blanket to sit on. If chairs are used, they need to be of a sort that allows one to sit up straight. Many of our physical exercises involve stretching out on the floor as well, so adequate floor space becomes an important consideration in selecting a room.

Little besides the cushions is needed in the way of material. Since we normally sit in a circle for our groups, we usually place a candle in the center of the room as another simple way of keeping our attention together. For many of us, the candle has become a symbol of the light we are seeking together. The lighting and extinguishing of the candle have also become signs of the beginning and ending of our meetings. On occasion some of our groups have used a flower or a leaf in the center of the circle. Our only suggestion in this regard is that if any accoutrements such as candles or flowers are used, they should be kept as simple as possible.

Size and Composition of Groups

In most cases the size and makeup of the group will be determined simply by who is interested in participating. But if over twenty possible participants are involved, more than one group should be planned and some care should be given to selection of members.

In general, we would suggest that groups be comprised of from four to twenty members. Groups of less than four have trouble if someone drops out or has to miss several sessions, and those with more than twenty become unwieldy and increasingly impersonal. An ideal size would be between eight and fifteen.

We have found it best to make groups as heterogenous and balanced as possible in terms of sex, denomination, vocation, etc. We especially emphasize having an equal or nearly equal number of men and women. The only exception that might be forseen to this principle of diversity would be those of marked cultural or theological differences (See Chapter 8). Our experience with adolescents has been limited, but in some cases it might be better for them to have a group of their own since their interests and attachments are often quite different from those of adults. On the other hand, some groups have found it very helpful to include young people, so this should be determined on an individual basis. A focus on silence together and on descriptions of developing interior experience are great "levellers"; differences in education, age, personality, etc., are hardly noticeable. However during more interpretive sharing time, differences reappear, usually in a mutually enriching way.

Process

After the initial clarification stages, a decision needs to be made as to who will be responsible for determining the ongoing content and process of the group. If the group is small and includes no one with prior experience in contemplative practice, it is probably necessary that the group itself plan its agenda for the duration of their meetings. This will require extra time which should be scheduled *in addition* to the regular meeting times. It is important that such planning activities not usurp the rhythm of the group meetings themselves.

A more efficient arrangement can be achieved if there are identified leaders for the group. As indicated in Chapter 2, the leaders would ideally be people who have had considerable contemplative experience as well as experience in group leadership, but even if no one meets these qualifications it is best to have someone identified as a leader. In general, we assume that a male-female leadership team would be the best arrangement. In any case, the leaders should assume the responsibility for planning, scheduling and carrying out the agenda of the meetings. They will select the topics, methods and approaches to be used, and will schedule and moderate evaluations and other administrative business. They will also be responsible for directing (or assigning the direction of) each phase of each group meeting; leading the physical exercise, presenting the chosen contemplative approach, ending the silence at the appropriate time, and initiating and moderating the discussion afterwards.

Even in a "leaderless" group, someone usually needs to be selected to begin and end the silence, and it is usually best if one person is designated to moderate the discussion. So a leaderless group would do well to plan, in advance, a schedule of rotating leadership so that someone is responsible for the conduct of each meeting.

If the planning of the agenda is done by the leaders, it will suffice that they put together a tentative schedule, review it with the group for comments and approval, and then proceed to implement it. This spares the group from wasting time and energy in planning activities. There may be situations in which members wish to have a greater voice in the planning and this will have to be worked out in each setting. The important principle here is that group time which could be spent in silence or reflection upon silence should not be given over to planning any more than is absolutely necessary. Even more importantly, both members and leaders should remember that all of their planning activities take place within the context of Divine Will. We are not the master planners.

At the beginning of each new group, there will be a tendency for the members to want to get to know each other and form some kind of group identity. While in other kinds of groups such activities constitute a vital part of the group process, we have come to feel that it is not so important for contemplative groups to engage in such activities. In fact, group identity and interpersonal emphases can sidetrack the group from its intent and waste considerable time and energy. We recommend that such activities be kept to a minimum during group meetings. Whatever interests the members have in social directions can be pursued on their own before or after meetings.

In beginning a group comprised of members who do not know each other, we have found it sufficient simply to go around the group and ask each person to give his or her name and perhaps a sentence or two about hopes or expectations. On other occasions when some total group sharing about a certain point is in order, it sometimes helps avoid extensive interpersonal concerns if members are asked to condense their feelings into one or two words. This also helps people simplify their thinking by cutting through extensive verbal discourse.

If a group is run in this way, it becomes even more important that some evaluation procedure be scheduled several times during the course of the group. This can be accomplished in a variety of ways. Participants may be asked to write down their evaluation, or special or extended meetings can be arranged in which evaluations can be discussed by the group as a whole. In any case, it is helpful for the leaders to prepare a series of questions to help people clarify their feelings. These should be simple questions such as "What are you finding helpful?" "What areas concern you?" "What do you feel needs to be added, subtracted or changed?" Similar simple questions can be asked about the participants' observations of positive and negative changes in themselves which might be related to their practice.

Some sort of evaluation process such as this should be undertaken in the middle and at the end of each group's span of meetings.

Spiritual Friends

The purpose and formation of spiritual friendships was discussed in Chapter 3. We feel these pairings should be set up as early as possible in the course of the group, perhaps even in advance of the group's first meeting. As previously discussed, we have found good results in randomized pairings, but if the leaders know something about the personalities and orientations of the participants in advance, they may wish to put some thought into matching people they think will complement each other. However, it is important to keep in mind that the ultimate value of the spiritual friendship will be determined by factors beyond the control of the leadership, and inevitably some pairings will hit it off well while others will not. Again, we recommend that pairing of males with females should take place whenever possible. The rationale behind this is explained in depth in Chapter 7. There may be some groups in which the members do not wish this cross-sexual pairing, so it should be discussed in the early planning and clarification stages if there is any doubt about it. Once the pairings have been made, it is wise to schedule time for them to meet together as soon as possible. It is good to arrange some time for this during the very first meeting, so that the foundations of the friendship can be established at the outset. During the first meeting of spiritual friends, it may help to give some simple instructions as to what might be discussed. Perhaps each pair could be asked to share their spiritual history with each other, to describe their conscious needs for spiritual deepening, or to go over some part of the self-search format together. A little structure such as this for their first meeting will help reduce social anxiety and minimize small talk.

As mentioned in Chapter 3, our suggestions for the ongoing relationships of the pairs include the following:

1. They are asked to keep each other in their prayers daily.
2. They are asked to work out their own arrangements for meeting outside the group if they so desire.
3. They are asked to keep their expectations of the relationship to a minimum, just being open to what comes.

Some group leaders suggest that the friend given them be received as a "gift," in order to help cultivate openness with each other.

Structure and Rhythm

While different groups may need different structures, it may be helpful to use the following as a model. Over a number of years, this schedule has become very consistent among our groups, and most of our participants have felt comfortable with its simplicity and reassured by its steadfastness.

Gathering (5-10 Minutes)

People often enter the building before the group is scheduled to begin. Some remain outside the room to converse or have coffee. Others enter and begin some silent settling down or Yoga. We have asked that silence be maintained in the meeting room so that people who wish to begin settling down early may do so without distraction. About the time the meeting is scheduled to begin the leader lights the candle and sits down, remaining quiet until everyone has gathered in the circle and made themselves comfortable.

Opening (1 Minute)

It is wise to have some simple ritualized activity in which everyone can participate to begin the meeting. After a short silence, we do this by slowly chanting "Shalom," initiated by the leader, with everyone bowing slightly towards the center of the circle as they intone the word. The meeting could just as well begin with a prayer or verse said or sung aloud together, or some silent gesture (holding hands, bowing heads, etc.). It is only important that everyone participate, and that the activity be short and simple. This procedure involves everyone in formally opening the meeting together.

Body Work (10-20 Minutes)

After the opening, the leader initiates some form of physical stretching, relaxing, or breathing exercises. In beginning groups it is best if the leader directs the members through each step of the sequence selected. Later, members can do this on their own. However, even in our longest term groups, members often ask that someone lead them through the exercises. There is a strength of community feeling that comes when everyone is doing the same thing, and people are likely to put more energy into activities which are led than into those which they are left to do on their own. This is important because the purpose of body work is to prepare for and in fact begin deeper silence by generating energy, alertness and vigor as well as relaxation.

There are innumerable varieties of physical activities which can be used for this purpose. We rely heavily on hatha yoga and yogic breathing. We have also drawn upon movements from Tai Chi, Aikido, self-massage such as the Tibetan Kum-nye, progressive muscular relaxation, balancing and centering exercises and even Sufi dancing (see Chapter 11).

It is important that sufficient time be given to this physical phase of silence, and that it include exercises which will help people stretch and relax as well as generate alertness and attentiveness. Slow, fluid movements and stillness should outweigh any jerky or quick movements. There is no need to strain in any of the exercises.

After the physical exercise the leader sits down in preparation for the silence, and this is a signal for the others to do likewise. At this point, everyone takes some time to get their spines in an upright position and to find a comfortable sitting position. Instruction in various sitting postures is given at the beginning of new groups.

Introduction to the Silence (5-10 Minutes)

According to the agenda previously worked out, the leader will initiate the specific contemplative method to be used that day. Usually he or she will say a few introductory words, reviewing the technique, relating it to previous weeks or themes, pointing out subtle variations which may occur, etc. If a new approach is being introduced the explanation may need to be fairly extensive. However, words and time should be kept to the minimum necessary so as not to interfere with the transition from physical relaxation into silence. Discussion at this point should be limited to questions of clarification by the members. After the leader explains what is necessary, the group begins the exercise. Again, there is a host of possibilities which range from chanting and visualizations to simple open silence. Examples will be given in Chapter 11.

The Silence (20-30 Minutes)

In very early meetings of beginning groups, the periods of silence may be no longer than 10 minutes, but very quickly, as the group feels comfortable with it, the time can be extended to twenty minutes. Later on, longer periods of time can be tried. During the silence with beginning groups, members can feel free to move if their bodies are uncomfortable, to cough or scratch an itch if they need to, or even to quit meditating and just sit quietly if the time seems too long for them. However, a person should notice the rise of such distractions and as s/he becomes used to silence learn more and more to let external stillness feed internal stillness, lightly letting go physical impulses to move and "pull out." The leader keeps time, and at the end softly claps his or her hands or rings a small bell.

Relaxation and Journal Writings (10-15 Minutes)

After the leader has signaled the end of the silence, participants come "out" of prayer or meditation slowly and gently. They may stretch, lie down, relax as they so desire. After some minutes of silent reflection, they may make some notes in their journals, or they may simply rest. No words are spoken during this time. We have found this "silence after the silence" to be a very important part of each meeting. It constitutes another more open and spontaneous form of meditation in and of itself. Some participants feel this is the most helpful part of each meeting for them. Especially those who can't keep from "trying too hard to meditate" find themselves finally relaxing and meditating during this time after the formal meditation is over. The leader usually ends this period when he or she senses that people are ready to begin some discussion.

Discussion and Reflection (30-40 Minutes)

The leader then opens the discussion period by asking if anyone has something to share. Since these are usually the first words to be spoken in 45 minutes or so, they are often said softly and with some difficulty, and there is often a considerable period of time before someone responds. Then the discussion begins, the leader simply serving to help clarify what people are trying to express. More experienced leaders may gently question interpretations of participants if they sense confusion, closedness, or rigidity in responses. During the discussion the leader needs to encourage a balance of talk about the immediate experience of the day, how people's personal practice is going, and the relationship between their practice and their daily lives. We generally attempt to address each of these three areas in one way or another during each meeting.

Closing (About 5 Minutes)

At the end of the meeting time, some administrative announcements or discussion may take place. Sometimes open intercessory prayer is offered. After this, the meeting is closed with a repeat of the opening "ritual," and the group adjourns. Again, socializing, coffee drinking, etc., are encouraged to take place outside the room in case someone wishes to remain in silence for a while.

During our monthly long sessions or when new approaches are introduced, the rhythm may be changed slightly from that described above, but we deviate very little from this standard form. We do feel that consistency in the rhythm is very helpful. Even more importantly, if we do make some changes we are very careful to preserve the time of open silence for 20-30 minutes in each meeting.

In summary, the process of beginning a group for the exploration of contemplative practice should include some very careful initial clarification of what it is that participants seek. Then care must be given to develop a clear and flexible structure within which the group can operate. This structure should include guidelines for attitudes, behavior and commitment of participants as well as scheduling and development of an agenda. Time for corporate open silence should receive the highest priority in each group meeting, as this is the heart of contemplative practice.

Some kind of leadership is necessary. It would of course be best to have as a leader someone who is experienced in both contemplative practice and group leadership. Where this is not feasible, the group should select someone to plan the agenda and moderate the meetings.

It is to be expected that anyone finding him/herself in the position of leading such a group will feel anxious about how they will do at it. It is always helpful for the leader to remember that he or she is simply serving to help establish and maintain an environment conducive to the group's mutual exploration and for the spirit's liberating movement. With common sense and a willingness not to hold to pretensions of responsibility for the members' spiritual growth, the leader will find it possible to pray for guidance and go about the work with a minimum of specialness and self-importance.

10

The Self-Search Format

An Instrument To Help People Clarify
Their Spiritual Journeys

The self-search format is an instrument devised by our study group to help people clarify their perceptions of their spiritual journeys. Its basic assumption is that by *clearly seeing* one's images of spirituality one can be more open to what seems to be needed and what directions one should take.

In the beginning the format had two objectives. The first was to generate useful data from Shalem group participants for our research project. The second was to provide an enriching experience for those participants. As we worked, the second objective grew in priority and rapidly broadened into the goal of developing an instrument which would be helpful for many people and in a variety of settings.

As part of our desire to generate useful data, we struggled with how to ask the kinds of questions which would cut through irrelevance and produce the clearest, simplest statements which would accurately reflect people's perceptions. Thus we finally arrived at the form of asking people, after each experience in the sequence, to respond to three questions about their spiritual journey:

117

1. What does it seem to be?
2. How does it seem to happen?
3. What seems to be needed now?

We found in general that as people progressed through the various exercises and experiences in the format, their answers to these questions became more simple, more concrete, and more practical. It seemed that a process was taking place through which layers of abstraction and verbal complexity were steadily stripped away. This was precisely what we wished would happen for our study, and it is precisely what we feel will be helpful to groups and individuals who wish to clarify their spiritual needs.

The process of developing, testing and refining this format was an exciting and sometimes difficult one. There was always the problem of over-objectification of people's spiritual experiences and feelings. And there were problems of confidentiality as well as many methodologic difficulties which had to be worked out. Some areas of the format, like the quotes, had to be revised several times before resulting in a useful form. As it stands now, the self-search format has been tested in a variety of groups and settings, and we feel it constitutes a rich resource for beginning long-term groups as well as for short-term experiences of spiritual clarification.

The following is the current format which we are using. Feel free to use all or parts of it as seems applicable to your situation. At the end we have included some alternatives which we tried at various points during the development of the format. You may use these as substitutes for other exercises in the sequence, or use them alone as needed.

Introduction to the Self-Search Format

Spirituality and religious formation may mean different things to different people. They may refer to one's personal experience of God, or of the most basic meaning of religion, one's clearest perceptions of life and its meaning, or one's deepest understanding of oneself. Perhaps spirituality and religious formation have to do with the experiences one has in prayer, meditation, worship, relationships or in nature or art. Or perhaps they relate to one's appreciation of consciousness or deepest sense of values. It is usually difficult to define spirituality and religious formation precisely, and this is perhaps as it should be.

The Spiritual Self-Search Format is not designed to produce a definition, but rather to provide some ways of getting in touch with and *learning from* your own inner sense of spiritual reality. Neither is this format designed to *produce* any specific religious experience. It is rather hoped to be a process of searching again and again into one's own personal experience in order to sense some directions and priorities which will help one live in deeper concordance and harmony with one's own basic truth.

Therefore, simply try to be open to yourself *as you are* in the process. Nurture an open, relaxed attitude without any special attempts to figure out or judge your experience or to worry about whether your experience is similar to or different from anyone else's. There will be an opportunity towards the end for you to draw some conclusions. In the meantime just be open and attentive to what happens.

In discussing your experience with others, simply express your thoughts, feelings and experiences as clearly and as personally as you can. It is impossible to describe spiritual experiences in words with total accuracy, but your attempts to do so may help to clarify your inner sense of those experiences. This is the purpose of the sharing. So there is no need to be concerned about agreement or consensus. For many people, personal spirituality is very private and delicate. Therefore be gentle and tactful, both in speaking and listening. No one should be pressed to express more than s/he feels comfortable with.

In sharing with others, continue your attitude of simply trying to be open and clear. Just try to understand. If you are listening to another person, simply try to understand what is being said. Ask questions which will help both of you clarify what is being said, but don't try to suggest things for the other person to do, and don't try to help them remedy their problems. If you simply try to understand, that in itself will be of help to them in their own understanding. Maintain an attitude of openness to and acceptance of the experiences of other people as well as your own.

General Outline of Spiritual Self-Search Format

I. INTRODUCTION

II. SILENCE
   1. Period of Silence
   2. Personal Reflection
   3. Share in triads
   4. Log

III. DRAW A PICTURE
Draw a picture which conveys your present experience of reality, of God, or of your sense of spiritual truth. It can take any form: realistic, abstract, or symbolic. Insofar as possible, let the picture "draw itself," and think about it after, not during the drawing process.

    1. Do it
    2. Share in triads
    3. Log

IV. LIFELINES
On a sheet of paper, draw a line representing your life. It may go up and down, back and forth, be jagged, curved, or straight. Place notations along the line to indicate significant events, changes, experiences or encounters which have altered or supported the direction of your life. Examine its directions, dimensions, turning points, and how you feel about them.

    1. Do it

Now, draw a line representing your *spiritual* life. Place notations along the line to indicate significant events, changes, experiences or encounters which have altered or supported the direction of your spiritual life. This line may be quite different from your lifeline, or it may be similar to or exactly the same as your lifeline. Examine its directions, dimensions, turning points, and how you feel about them.

    1. Do it
    2. Share in triads
    3. Log

V. SPIRITUAL GIANTS OF YOUR PAST

Step I
Brainstorm all the people who have been influential in your life, spiritually. (5 minutes) Go over your entire list and pick the three most important to you right *now*. Write down some reasons why these have emerged on top. (10 minutes)

Step II
Pick one of these three. Write out some factual information about this person. Then, begin writing a dialogue with this person. (30 minutes)

1. Do it
2. Share in triads
3. Log

VI. FOLLOW THE DIRECTIONS ON PAGES 122-123.

Step I
Choose the one quote which speaks most to your state of mind *now*; choose the one that seems most alien to you now; choose the one which expresses where you *wish* you were now in your journey. Identify your perception of why you react to these particular quotes in each of these ways.

Step II
Jot down fantasies about what you imagine the writer of the quote which speaks the most to you is like. Dialogue with the quote or fantasy.

1. Do it
2. Share in triads
3. Log

VII. A SEARCH FOR THE FUTURE
Taking some individual time to review what has happened this day. Make some notes as to what the experiences and reflections seem to be telling you. Consider any sense of direction, needs, possible future steps.

1. Do it
2. In triads share to the extent that you comfortably can what you have realized today that you can rejoice in; what you have heard today that concerns you.

VIII. COMMENT ON THE EXPERIENCE
1. Spiritual Growth: What does it seem to be? How does it seem to happen? What needs do you perceive you have for the present?

2. In reflection upon your spiritual journey, were there some surprises, i.e., any new learnings, for you? If so, list a few.
3. Have your perceptions of your spiritual life changed as a result of this experience? Share as much about the change as feels comfortable.
4. Which experiences were most and least significant, and how?
5. Any other comments or suggestions.

Quotes

I. The following are a series of quotations taken from a wide variety of sources in world literature. After you have read them all, go back over them and pick two which most closely represent the kind of spirituality that is most appealing to you.*

1. "Yet when the years have rolled past . . . men and women will know and children will be taught that we have a finer land, a better people, a more noble civilization—because these humble children of God were willing to suffer for righteousness' sake."
2. "We all ought to love prayer as the body loves the soul. And just as the body cannot live without the soul, so the soul cannot live without prayer. And insofar as a person prays as he ought to pray, he does well. He will not walk, he will run in the ways of the Lord, and will be raised to a high degree of the love of God."
3. "A man has many skins in himself, covering the depths of his heart. Man knows so many things, he does not know himself. Why, thirty or forty skins or hides, just like an ox or a bear's, so thick and hard, cover the soul. Go into your own ground and learn to know yourself there."
4. "By love I do not mean any natural tenderness, which is more or less in people according to their constitution: But I mean a larger principle of the soul, founded in reason and piety, which makes us tender, kind and gentle to all our fellow creatures as creatures of God, and for his sake."
5. "In prayer he did not stop at the frontiers of his knowledge and his reasoning. He adored God and his mysteries as they are in themselves and not as he understood them."
6. "With the lamp of word and discrimination one must go beyond word and discrimination and enter the path of realization."

II. Once you have chosen two quotes, take a few minutes reflection

---

*The first quote is from Martin Luther King's Nobel acceptance speech. Quotations 2 through 6 were taken from THE PERENNIAL PHILOSOPHY, by Aldous Huxley, Harper and Row, N.Y., 1970. *Quotes*: 1. Martin Luther King, Jr., 2. St. John of the Cross, 3. Eckhart, Meister, p. 162, 4. Law, William, p. 85, 5. Amelote, p. 223, 6. Lankavatara Sutra, p. 133.

time, and jot a few notes to yourself on why the quotes you chose had greater appeal to you than others.

Do not read Step III until you have done Step I and II.

III. The quotes listed above are rough estimations of three different approaches to spirituality:

1. *The Way of Knowing* (The True)
Either Scientific, Theological, Philosophical
Scholarly knowing or intuitive knowing found in mysticism or psychic powers

2. *The Way of Action* (The Good)
Personal and corporate moral action
Caring for the world
Being for your neighbor
Healing

3. *The Way of Prayer and Adoration* (The Beautiful)
Intense personal worship
Anything related to beauty
Poetry, Art, etc.

If you found quotes 3 and 6 appealing, you have a greater propensity for the *Way of Knowing* as a spiritual path.

If quotes 1 and 4 were more attractive, then the *Way of Action* has a greater appeal as a spiritual path.

If quotes 2 and 5 were your choice, then the spiritual *Way of Prayer and Adoration* has greater appeal to you.

If you discovered your choices falling within two categories, perhaps you are open to several ways of growing and maturing spiritually. On the other hand it could indicate some internal ambivalence you feel regarding which is most important.

Try to steer clear of placing value judgments on whether your choices are good or bad. All three paths have been affirmed for centuries by spiritual giants of the present and past. Instead, try to enter into a reflective mode as to why one path has greater significance to you now than another. Does your choice reflect your spiritual roots? What else is the source of your choice? How open are you to growth in other paths?

Take a few minutes to jot some notes to yourself regarding your thoughts on these matters.

IV. Meet with your trio to share your reflections and insights.

V. Spend a few minutes by yourself again to write down the things you have learned from this particular exercise.

Instructions To The Triads

Within each triad, each person has an assigned role. The three roles are Speaker, Listener, and Observer. Within the time limit, each individual should have an opportunity to share his or her material with a Listener. This requires that the role cards be passed around so that each person in the triad has an opportunity to perform each role once. The instructions on the role cards should facilitate your task.

The following should be reproduced on 4 x 6 index cards:

THE SPEAKER

Your Task:

Put your thoughts, feelings, experiences, into words so they will be understandable to another.

Be as specific and personal as is comfortable. It will be helpful to you and to those listening to avoid generalities and impersonal abstractions.

Note what you say with interest and curiosity. Try not to be judgmental about your own material. Insight and understanding may follow later. You may be surprised at how it all gets put together.

THE LISTENER

Your Task:

To assist the speaker to be as clear and precise about his/her story or material as possible.

The following questions may help clarify their message:
"Could you say more about . . .?"
"What do you mean by . . .?"
"Is there anything else you can tell me about . . .?"

Avoid:
Judgmental or evaluative statements
Giving advice
Interjecting your experience or insights into the process
These would most likely stop or hinder the flow of consciousness or train of thought of the speaker.

THE OBSERVER

Your Task:

To observe and facilitate the process. Concentrate less on *what* is being said and more on *how* the persons are interacting.
> What helps them communicate?
> What blocks their communication?

As the Observer you will:
—not normally speak until the discussion is complete
—intervene if guidelines are not being followed
—share your perceptions about the process after the discussion is complete without getting into the content of the interview
—be tactful in giving feedback
It's hard being an Observer. The content is probably engaging and inviting. Resist the temptation. Your role as process observer is important to this whole design.

Alternatives

On the following pages you will find alternative activities that can be used to replace or supplement the activities listed in the Self-Search Format.

As with the Self-Search Format, be sure that after each led experience the participants answer the three questions discussed earlier in this chapter about the nature of their spiritual journeys:

1. What it seems to be
2. How it seems to happen
3. What seems to be needed now

Alternative I

The Word That Speaks to Us Now

STEP ONE (30 minutes)
> By memory, make a random listing of the words, phrases, passages that have special meaning for you. If you can't remember the exact words, make do with what you can remember.

You will want to place on this list things that have sustained you in the past, or given you hope, or helped shape the direction of your religious journey.

These can be favorite sayings, phrases or lines from hymns, liturgies or scripture, or quotes from others. Make the list as long as possible within the allotted time.

STEP TWO (5 minutes)
Go back over your list now. Pick out the ones that have special meaning to you at this moment. Which one speaks to the way you have been feeling most recently?

STEP THREE (10 minutes)
Your top three choices may be an indication of where you are currently in your spiritual journey. Using this material, take a few minutes now to write a few lines describing your current journey.

What makes these passages particularly significant to you now? How do they relate to the issues you are currently facing in your life? How do they relate to your past? Can you use the material to project into future dimensions of your pilgrimage?

Give your interpretation of the meaning of your top 3 choices.

Alternative II

Throughout history, people usually had the opportunity to check their individual religious experience against the experience and understanding of a larger community. At times this was a point of tension, as those with special insight, vision or prophetic utterance found themselves in conflict with the larger community. Over the long pull, however, this process has been able to caution or discourage those pursuing blind alleys or following false spirits and to encourage things that lead to wholeness and spiritual health.

In short, the religious community as a body has an important function to play in relation to individual spiritual growth.

By way of this community today being helpful to individuals, take 5 minutes with some paper and write out one or two things that concern you about what you've heard or observed today. Limit your remarks to the area of spiritual belief or practice. An evaluation of the day will take place at a later time.

Your comments will be collated and read to the group later today. Your identity will be guarded.

Alternative III

The Spiritual Lifeline

This is a pencil-and-paper exercise for exploring the development and dimensions of an individual's spiritual life. It is based on models developed by Herbert Shepard ("Planning for Living") and Tilden Edwards. It can be used to explore yourself, or as a means of assisting others.

Instructions

PART I
On a sheet of paper, draw a line representing your spiritual life. It may go up and down, back and forth, be jagged, curved, or straight. Put an "X" on the end of the line to represent where you are now. Place notations along the line to indicate significant events, changes, experiences or encounters which have altered or supported the direction of the line. Examine its directions, dimensions, turning points, and how you feel about them.

PART II
1. Continue on from the "X" with a dotted line, to indicate where you wish the line to go in the future.
2. Continue on from the "X" with a solid line, where you *really* expect it to go.
3. Examine the two lines: What are the differences? What will account for the differences, or lack thereof? What feelings, ideas, hopes, or plans can you experience in terms of where the lines head?

PART III
Share your experience with another.

Alternative IV

Blocks to Spiritual Awareness and Practice

INSTRUCTIONS: First, write down some of your own thoughts about the kinds of things which seem to get in the way of prayer, worship, meditation, or otherwise impede your development of spiritual awareness. Secondly, go over the list, checking those items which apply to you. See if you can think of any others. Next, write some comments about these blocks, see if you can find a pattern in them, or get in touch with some reasons which may underly them. Finally, share your findings and reactions with another.

— No problems at all
— Can't find the time
— Other, more important things
— Fear of losing control
— Too tired usually
— Can't concentrate
— Feel tense, worried, afraid
— Experience bad feelings/images
— Sleep during prayer/meditation
— Embarrassment, self-consciousness
— Not comfortable physically
— Not comfortable mentally
— Can't stop thinking
— Fear of Evil, the Occult
— Need to be logical, to understand
— Bad feelings about myself
— Fear of losing touch with myself
— Can't give up my own will or need to control things
— Fear of being tricked/fooled
— Fear of death
— Anger at church, God, religion
— Fear of God's judgment
— Fear of God's demands
— Fear that God won't be there
— Bad feelings about others
— Fear of using Religion as an escape
— Need to be *doing* something/can't just sit still
— Get physical symptoms
— Children, family demands
— Feel selfish
— Disbelief that God is a "Person" to be "talked" or "listened" to
— Overfascination with certain experiences/can't get beyond them
— Impatience

— Can't think of words to pray
— Feel childish/immature
— Afraid of failure
— Don't know what I want
— Spiritual feelings slip away
— Feel no spiritual needs
— Fear of feeling "holier than thou"
— Get bored/restless
— Don't trust spiritual leaders
— Fear of changing personality
— Fear of changing values
— Fear of going crazy
— Fear of fanaticism
— It's too much work
— Never get any results
— Can't "just be"
— Bad mood afterwards
— Too much on my mind
— Fear of getting too emotional
— Fear of giving up other things
— Scary experiences
— Fear of losing faith
— Fear of evangelism
— Rebellion against the "shoulds" and "oughts" of religion
— Haven't really been trying
— Belief that man cannot help himself spiritually . . . only God can
— Too many distractions
— Feeling lonely, no support from others
— Don't know how to do it
— Guilt or shame
— Can't discipline self
— Pride gets in way of admitting any spiritual awareness needs
— Fear of being changed
— Rebellion against religious language

11

Methods

Specific Suggestions for the Establishment and Conduct of Contemplative Practice

There are so many styles of contemplative practice available that it is very difficult to know which to choose. Every group will probably have to go through some trial-and-error processes before a few approaches are found which seem worth exploring in depth. During our beginning groups we present a "cafeteria" of different styles and techniques, thus exposing participants to a variety of approaches from which to choose. Then during subsequent years we encourage simplification and greater depth. The danger of a cafeteria approach is that people may be tempted to sample a number of methods superficially without moving into any in depth. On the other hand, some variety is necessary for people to find a style with which they are comfortable. This balance between variety and depth is a critical one, especially during the first year, and each group should address it honestly.

Space prohibits a full description of all the approaches we have used, and the reader is encouraged to review the two books which deal more specifically with our techniques.* What will be offered in this

---

*Edwards, T. *Living Simply Through the Day*, Paulist Press, New York, 1977.
May, G. *The Open Way*, Paulist Press, New York, 1977.

chapter is an overview of our approaches with selected examples and basic principles. These should suffice to provide a practical grounding in methods to which other resources can be added.

Perhaps the most basic and important principal to keep in mind is that the goal of any contemplative technique should be to create *openness and clarity*. It should help the individual relax his or her grip on preconceptions and prejudices, and it should foster a combination of alertness and relaxation. In practice this means things should be kept as simple as possible and techniques which add a great deal of material or complexity to consciousness should be avoided. Similarly, we do not recommend using techniques which induce trances, prolonged fantasy or other dramatic experiences which tend to capture one's attention or close one off from immediate reality as-it-is-happening-here-and-now. We are not seeking exciting mystical experience. What we are seeking is simple open receptivity to God.

As with certain schools of Buddhism and contemplative Christianity, our sense is that the best form of prayer or meditation is simply to sit in the presence of God, just being open and receptive, neither adding to nor subtracting from what God gives us in that moment.

The problem is that one often has difficulty getting "to" this simple, open and accepting state of mind. More often than not one's mind seems cluttered, filled, attached to this or that preoccupation, holding, grasping, fleeing and struggling. The value of "techniques" of contemplative practice, then, is to help the individual cut through all this clutter so that the open state of mind can more easily occur. Five basic activities help this process.

Principles for Formal Contemplative Practice

There are three basic principles which facilitate times of formal contemplative prayer and meditation:

A. Body Work

Stretching, breathing, relaxing and balancing exercises help to promote physical relaxation and easing of tension, which in turn invariably help ease mental tension. At the same time, done properly, such activities help release energy and promote alertness and attentiveness as preparation for sitting in silence.

B. A Centering Process for Attention

Giving the mind a simple, central object or activity to pay attention to during the silence provides a kind of "home base" or central landmark which can greatly assist the process of letting the mind quiet down and become more open. We do not advocate strict or forceful concentration on the object or focus of meditation. This often creates needless additional stress and work. Rather, we recommend a gentle "interest" in the focus, allowing the mind to roam if it so desires, but gently and repeatedly bringing one's attention back. In this way the mind slowly calms down and relaxes.

C. Simple Waiting

Perhaps more important than the other two factors, the simple practice of just sitting, waiting, and remaining attentive serves to give the mind its needed time to become relaxed and clear. This process cannot be rushed, and it requires considerable patience and gentleness with oneself.

Principles for Informal Contemplative Practice

The preceding three factors apply to the actual practice of formal contemplative prayer and meditation, which of course occupies a small percentage of one's time each day. There are two other activities which we encourage to take place during the rest of daily living, when people are not engaged in formal prayer and meditation:

Attentiveness

This is the simple practice of trying to stay as immediately aware as possible in all the things one does during the course of a day. Whether working, eating, talking, playing or thinking, the individual attempts to remain conscious of what is going on in the immediate moment. This again encourages a "centering down" of attention and a minimization of mental clutter. In doing this, perception becomes somewhat clearer and one increasingly senses the sacredness of each moment in life.

Journal Keeping

The practice of making regular written notes of one's experiences, feelings, perceptions and hopes provides additional structure and momentum for one's practice. The journal can be a very helpful way of exploring and clarifying one's experience as well as recording the ups and downs of practice. It encourages attentiveness and consistency in whatever one does.

There are other activities which we encourage, such as the reading of scripture and contemplative literature, personal retreats, poustinias and pilgrimages, exploration of fasting and other ascetic disciplines, and the practice of compassionate action. But these five main undertakings constitute the body of our work, and for this reason each will be discussed in some depth.

Principles for Formal Contemplative Meditation

Body Work

As preparation for silence or as a means of encouraging attentiveness through the day, nothing is more helpful than spending some time in physical activity. There are three basic aspects to body work in contemplative practice. The first is simple *body awareness*, becoming immediately aware of the body as an integrated part of one's existence. This awareness occurs with any physical activity, but is especially encouraged by activities which promote a sense of balance and fluidity of movement. The second is *relaxation and release of energy*, best exemplified by the stretching/relaxing rhythm of Hatha Yoga. The third is *breathing*, which facilitates the other two and provides ongoing awareness of the dynamic processes of life. Since breathing is such an integral part of all body work, some examples of breathing exercises will be given first.

BREATHING. The most basic practice of breathing is simply taking slow, deep, full breaths. It is good to spend several minutes with this simple breathing, allowing it to be as smooth and fluid as possible, sensing alertness and vigor during inhalation, allowing all one's muscles to relax during exhalation. There are innumerable refinements and elaborations of this basic breathing which can be found in books on Hatha Yoga. Beginning groups often find it helpful to breathe in and out in rhythm together, with the leader setting the pace verbally or with movements of his or her hands.

Another good practice with breathing is to spend a few minutes simply being aware of breathing without attempting to control it in any way. People usually find it difficult to do this in the beginning, but become more adept with practice. This encourages the kind of gentle, nonmanipulative observation which is necessary during open prayer or meditation.

BODY AWARENESS. A basic body awareness exercise begins standing upright, feet about shoulder width apart, knees slightly bent and shoulders relaxed. In this position one senses the basic balance and symmetry of the body, its rootedness to the ground, its capacity for becoming very still. One also naturally becomes aware of one's breathing, and its rhythm in the stillness. After a few minutes of motionless relaxation in this position, a sense of balance can be enhanced by very slowly shifting one's weight back and forth from one foot to the other. If desired, this movement can be expanded into slow walking around the room, staying relaxed and balanced all the while. There may be times, when the atmosphere seems unusually heavy or lethargic, that it is helpful to speed up the movements, adding some swinging of the arms or even jumping up and down. This raises the energy and alertness of the group and takes care of any impending sleepiness. But before settling down for silence it is always best to slow down the movements and make them more gentle and fluid.

Sometimes it suffices simply to move one or two parts of the body. For example, the head can slowly be rolled around in a circle, down towards one shoulder, then forwards toward the chest, around to the other shoulder, then stretched backwards and on to the first shoulder again. This movement is repeated several times, slowly, gently, perhaps in time with one's breathing. Then the direction of the movement is reversed for a similar period of time. Or participants can sit comfortably and simply move their hands slowly around in the air, sensing the forms they make, the space between and around them, the smoothness and beauty of their motion. In any case it is important that people pay attention to the sensations of their bodies during this time, and try to get a sense of being in tune with the physical part of themselves without undue fascination.

Another good body-awareness practice is the self-massage of one or more parts of the body. We have found that some time spent carefully massaging one's face, head or feet is very helpful in stimulating energy as well as body awareness and relaxation. The massage should be gentle but firm, and if tender areas are encountered one should relax and breathe deeply rather than tense up with the pain.

RELAXATION AND RELEASE OF ENERGY. As indicated

above, Hatha Yoga is the best practice for relaxing and energizing the body. Hatha Yoga is a very refined system of stretching and relaxing which is done in harmony with breathing, and its overall effect is an excellent preparation for silent prayer and meditation.

There are many good books and readily available classes on Hatha Yoga, and prospective group leaders are encouraged to learn some Yoga postures from such resources if they have not already done so. In our groups, we rely heavily on basic Yoga as the primary preparation for silence. Two simple practices will be described here as examples.

A STRETCHING/RELAXING EXERCISE FOR THE WHOLE BODY. The participants lie on their backs on the floor, arms at sides, legs slightly separated, and begin some slow, deep abdominal breathing. The stomach should rise towards the ceiling during inhalation and press down towards the floor during exhalation. Sometimes it is helpful to place a hand on the stomach to increase one's awareness of this pattern. During each exhalation, the participants allow their muscles to relax, especially those in arms and legs. Sometimes sighing a little as one breathes out helps to encourage this relaxation.

After a few minutes of this breathing and relaxing, the leader instructs the group to take a very deep, slow breath, and while doing so to raise their right arms slowly up over their heads. They then hold their breath and stretch their arms, hands and fingers way back over their heads as far as possible. Then, together on the leader's signal, they slowly exhale and let their arms swing slowly back down to the side, finally letting them rest on the floor, very relaxed. After a few moments the same exercise is repeated with the left arm. Then the right leg is stretched, with toes pointed and foot curled down, and then relaxed, with the breathing. Then the same with the left leg. After this, both arms are stretched together in the same way, followed by both legs, and finally both arms and legs together, so that the entire body gets a good healthy stretch. Each of these stretches is coordinated with breathing. This is followed by a time of just lying still on the floor, breathing normally, and being aware of how the body and mind feel. Then *very* slowly, the group can rise to a seated position.

A PREPARATION FOR SITTING. The group begins by sitting on the floor, legs together straight out in front, spine upright. A deep breath is taken in, and as it is exhaled, they slowly bend forward at the waist, sliding their hands down their legs as far as possible without pain. They remain in this bent-forward position for a few more breaths, going just a little further as they relax more with each exhalation. Then, on an inhalation, they slowly sit up straight again and spread their legs as far apart on the floor as is comfortable. The exercise is repeated twice, first sliding down the right leg, then the left.

Then, on assuming an upright sitting position with the left leg out straight on the floor, the right leg is bent so that the right foot can be placed on top of the left thigh. Breathing out slowly, the right knee is pressed down towards the floor by pushing with the hands or leaning forward on it with the right elbow. This stretches the hip joint and helps prepare the individual for prolonged cross-legged sitting. The exercise is then repeated on the opposite side, after which the individual sits upon a cushion and crosses the legs as comfortably as possible.

It is not essential for contemplative groups to sit on the floor, and many people may find it uncomfortable to do so at first. But we have found it helpful to encourage sitting on the floor rather than in chairs whenever possible. In part this is because people habitually tend to dull their awareness a bit when sitting in a chair or lying down. Practicing contemplative prayer or meditation in a rather "special" position, one which is not usually associated with other activities such as talking, sleeping or watching TV simply helps encourage alertness and attentiveness throughout the periods of silence. Though this may seem like a small point, such little factors can make the difference between a bright, clear and open period of meditation, and a heavy period of lethargy.

The Centering Process

Once the body has had its time of energizing and relaxing, a similar process can take place with the mind. In order for a state of openness and clarity to occur, the noisy activity of the mind needs to settle down. Work with the body will facilitate this automatically, but usually some additional ways of quieting the mind are needed. Here there is a very important principle to remember; *attempts to make the mind quiet by force are likely to create even more mental noise and may in fact be dangerous*. Thus we discourage forceful attempts to concentrate on one thing or effortful attempts to exclude or shut down thinking.

The emphasis, rather, is on gentle, consistent and diligent watchfulness of the mind, allowing it to "go off" on sidetracks without struggle, but gently and repeatedly returning it to some central base for attention. With this gentle, repeated pattern the mind slowly settles of its own accord, and openness simply is what is left after the noise quiets down. Nothing is held on to or pushed away; no struggle is added to the mind; judgments and expectations are held to a minimum; and one is very patient and accepting of the troublesomeness of one's mind.

The importance of this kind of attitude cannot be overemphasized. Unless leadership is extremely competent in spiritual practice, we advise against the use of any effort or force in contemplative practice.

In order to provide a "home base" for attention to which the mind can return after it wanders, some object, image, thought or activity must be selected. Here one needs to spend some time experimenting with different bases until one or two are found which seem worthy of moving into in depth. Almost anything can be used as a base for attention in this manner. One might look at a candle flame, a flower or the leaves on a tree. Or one might repeat a word, sound, prayer or short piece of scripture silently in one's mind. Or one can create a mental-visual image and pay attention to that. Or one can simply listen to the sounds occurring in the environment, allowing them to come and go as they will.

The selection of a base for meditation should be undertaken with some care, because the base will tend to determine the overall atmosphere of the silence. In this sense, groups which wish to maintain a very specifically Christian atmosphere may want to choose a cross or an image of Christ, New Testament scripture excerpts, the Jesus Prayer or other similar items for bases. Jewish groups may want to explore traditional Jewish meditations which use a candle flame and/or visualizations of Hebrew letters as bases. More eclectic groups may wish to draw from Buddhist and Hindu mantras and mandalas, or utilize things from nature.*

Whatever is chosen as a base, it is *gently* "planted" in one's attention and is held very loosely and delicately. The most common mistake made by beginners in this practice is to try to hold on to the base with too much effort. People often assume that by such forceful holding of attention they can compel their minds to become quiet. But usually this simply results in fatigue and frustration. It is important to remind the group repeatedly that no special effort is needed in this regard; that the practice is one of gentleness, relaxation and patience. When the mind wanders, *it is allowed to do so*. Then, when it seems "finished" with its wandering, when there is no struggle, attention can be brought back to the base with no effort at all.

Two of the most popular bases in our groups have been breathing and chanting, and they will be discussed in some detail as examples.

Breathing. The group is seated on the floor, spines upright, after a period of physical stretching and relaxation. The participants are instructed to allow their shoulders, faces and stomach muscles to relax,

The Open Way, G. May, Paulist Press, New York, 1977.

and simply become aware of their breathing. The simplest breathing-base is just to be attentive to the breath as it comes in and out, not controlling it, but just bringing the mind back to the breathing whenever it has wandered.

Beginners often find this simple practice too subtle, and need a stronger activity for a base. In this case, the group can be instructed to count each exhalation silently, from one to three. After three exhalations, the counting begins at one again and this process is repeated throughout the silence. Or some words or sounds can be said silently in the mind to help maintain attentiveness. For example, one can silently think "In . . . Out . . . In . . . Out . . ." as one breathes. Or the Jesus Prayer can be set silently to the rhythm of breathing, praying "Lord Jesus Christ" during the inhalation and "Have mercy upon me" on the exhalation.

Chanting. Chanting aloud is a very good way for groups to begin a period of silence. There is a strong feeling of community in making sound together, and considerable alertness and energy seem to be generated. Similarly, a period of chanting can be very helpful in centering attention and quieting extraneous mental chatter. Again, there is an endless variety of words, sounds and phrases which can be used for chanting. The Jesus Prayer or any other short prayer can be said or sung aloud together. Single words such as "Peace," "Holy," "Amen," "Shalom," or "Alleluia" can be intoned. Or single syllables such as "OM," "AH," or "HUM" can be used. With longer phrases it is best if the group chants them in unison and synchrony, following a rhythm established by the leader. With short words or sounds, the same practice can be followed or each individual in the group can intone the word at his or her own pace and rhythm. This produces a constant rising and falling sound in the group as a whole.

During the chanting, the sounds should be made easily, comfortably, usually at a low pitch with full breath and deep resonance. One should give oneself to the sound, but fanciness and entertainment should be avoided. It is helpful to encourage the group to "let" the sound come rather than try to "make" it, to go with it and follow its lead, without being too concerned about pitch or volume.

The period of chanting should last for at least five minutes, but may go on much longer. It may be allowed to stop of its own accord or the leader may stop it abruptly with a clap of his or her hands. In either case, the group remains attentive to the silence after the sound stops, and may use the mental reverberations of the sound as a base for attention during the rest of the silence.

Simple Waiting

During the main period of silence, whether a base for attention is used or not, the individual should cultivate an attitude of patient, open receptivity. In this attitude, expectations are minimized and one is very accepting of any thoughts, sounds, images or other stimuli which come into consciousness. One does not attempt to judge, name or otherwise evaluate what comes to mind but rather sits like a transparent, empty channel through which all thoughts and sensations simply come and go. Tarthang Tulku calls this attitude "Nothing holding anything anywhere." It is simply the allowing and seeing of whatever comes to mind. External sounds which in other settings might be seen as distractions are simply part of the experience of the moment. No attempt is made either to shut them out or to cling to them. The same is true of all internal thoughts, images or sensations, no matter how dramatic they may seem. They are simply allowed to come and go, rise and fall of their own accord.

In the midst of this coming-and-going of thoughts and sensations one sits very still, unmoved, uninfluenced by whatever is taking place but sharply aware of it. *Thus the proper contemplative state here is not necessarily one in which the mind shuts down and all thoughts and sensations cease. Rather it is an inner solidity of attentiveness in the midst of whatever is happening.*

Sometimes this attitude can be helped by beginning the period of silence with a prayer in which the Divine is asked to watch over and to protect the individual during the time of openness. Then, with an attitude of "Thy Will Be Done," the entire period of silence, with whatever experiences it may bring, is offered up to God. This assists the individual in easing his or her own expectations and judgments about the experiences encountered in silence.

But most importantly, one needs to wait. Quietly, neither pushing nor pulling, neither shutting out nor clinging, one simply and attentively waits.

Principles for Informal Practice

As mentioned above, attentiveness and journal-keeping are practices specifically designed to take place when one is *not* involved in formal contemplative prayer or meditation. Together they help to build a bridge of consistency between the times of formal silence and the rest of one's daily life.

Attentiveness

Called "mindfulness" or "witnessing" in Eastern religious traditions, attentiveness means to be as immediately aware as possible all
through the day, in everything one does. Attentiveness encourages a
present-centeredness in which one's awareness is open to what is happening right here and now rather than being caught up by concerns of
past or future. This is not to say that past and future should not be
thought about, but rather that such thoughts should not *remove or hinder*
one's awareness of the present and should be recognized as taking place
in the present. Such present-centered attentiveness helps to keep one in
an open and receptive frame of mind more of the time. Blind reflexive
action and behavior stemming from attachment to desire and fear-
images are minimized. And one has the opportunity to sense the wonder
and sanctity of each moment of daily life.

There are several ways to facilitate daily attentiveness. A short
prayer, word, sound or Koan* can be kept going constantly in one's
mind, as a reminder to be present. Or one can develop the habit of
becoming aware of breathing during all activities. Similarly if one
changes one's habits slightly, such as wearing a watch on the opposite
wrist or a ring on a different finger, the feeling of strangeness associated
with this change can serve as a signal to "watch what's happening now."
Fasting and other ascetic practices which produce a *mild* feeling of
dis-satisfaction can also be used as reminders.

More helpful than any of these is the development of a habitual
"watching" of what one is doing. For example when one is walking,
talking, driving, eating, working, etc., a small part of consciousness can
be set aside as an observer of these actions. In the beginning people often
find it helpful to comment silently to themselves about what is going on.
"Here I am, sitting and reading," or "Here I am driving the car," etc.
Later, as the habit of observation becomes more familiar, the silent
verbal comment can be dropped and activities at hand can simply be
noticed.

Whenever this observation takes place, it is important that it not
become critical or judgmental. It is often people's tendency to follow
"Here I am, doing this" with "How well am I doing this?" or "Should I
be doing this?" Such judgmental discourse becomes caught up by evaluation. So the observation or witnessing of present happenings needs to
be kept as free from judgment as possible. Normal judgment and evaluation can take place as needed, but they must be seen as *part of* the

---

*See Chapter 4.

happenings of the present moment rather than as factors which draw attention *away* from that moment.

Consciousness of body movements, especially when walking, exercising or working with the hands, can help facilitate present-centered attentiveness. So can periodic attention to the senses. "What am I seeing now? Feeling? Touching? Hearing? Thinking?" All of these activities serve to deepen one's appreciation of life as-it-is-happening and in turn facilitate one's capacity to be attentive and accepting in periods of silent prayer and meditation. The practice of regular or continuing intercessory prayer during daily activities can also greatly facilitate attentiveness, while at the same time minimizing the likelihood of this attentiveness becoming too self-centered.

It might be said that one of the goals of contemplative practice is for every behavior, every moment, every thought to become an act of prayer. With a balance between open acceptance during silence and attentiveness during activity, the individual's mind moves more and more in this direction.

Journal Keeping

The maintenance of a journal fulfills several needs. First it provides a sense of structure, continuity and direction for one's personal pilgrimage. Second, it offers a way of clarifying and integrating the experiences one has had in contemplative practice and daily life. Third, it provides an additional source of accountability and encouragement to continue practice.

Some people find journal writing very easy, while for others it seems like a burden requiring excessive time and energy. We would recommend that members of beginning groups be encouraged to keep a journal at least for several months, until they have an adequate opportunity to evaluate its worth for them.

A journal is not a diary. While a diary is simply a daily log of experiences, a journal is an active, dynamic process in which one takes part. The journal should be a place where people can think things through on paper as well as record events. It should be a means of self-exploration as well as an accounting of experience.

Some people will want to spend time each day working with their journals. Others may choose to write only when they feel moved to do so. One member of our groups chose to draw a mandala each day rather than write in her journal. Others decided to make their journal entries in the form of written prayers. Still others wrote poetry, or related their journal entries to daily scriptural readings. Many group members chose to follow the journal-keeping style of Ira Progoff.* Whatever form is used, there should be enough flexibility to allow for those individual variations and for experimentation with differing uses.

If the journal proves to be a help to group members, then they may be encouraged to keep their notes in a small book which they can carry around with them at all times. And certainly each group meeting should offer time after the silence to be used for journal notations if people so desire.

---

*Ira Progoff, AT A JOURNAL WORKSHOP, Dialogue House, N.Y., 1975.

Part IV

Perspective and Critique

12

Voices of Authority

Interviews With Twenty-Nine Spiritual Leaders and Groups

Most of the material in this book has been gleaned from examination of our own experience and that of the people who have participated with us as group members. As a balance to this, and to broaden and check our own perspectives, we were privileged to interview a large number of other people. We have chosen to call this group of people "spiritual leaders," though not all truly fit into that category and most would be uncomfortable with that title. We have even gone so far as to call their insights "Voices of Authority," because we feel each of them has demonstrated some particular experiential maturity in an intuitive, contemplative path.

The choice of whom to interview was not based on arbitrary criteria, for as we have discussed in Chapter 2, the qualities of spiritual leadership are difficult to discern and probably impossible to quantify. I suppose each of us has some stereotyped image of what a true spiritual leader would be like. The image is usually that of the saintly guru, completely realized, with no lingering ego attachments or needs for gratification of personal desire to get "in the way" of Divine wisdom. Our interviews, not surprisingly, bore out that few such individuals exist today in the roles of carefully trained spiritual leaders. On the other hand, we were deeply encouraged by the large number of persons who do express qualities of sincere and dedicated spiritual leadership; persons both well-known and obscure, educated and uneducated, scattered through all peoples. As our interviews progressed, many more people came to our attention whom we would have liked to meet, but could not because of time or economic limitations. It was thus both frustrating and heartening to discover the vast wealth of spiritual resources which exists today in people all over the world.

Our initial intent was to interview a few leaders whom we had already met or heard of who seemed to demonstrate particular expertise in traditions similar to our own contemplative paths. Such persons represent the bulk of the interviewees; mostly Christian, but also including a few Jewish and Buddhist leaders. But over the months other people came to our attention and were added to the list, some of whom represented rather differing traditions. These included a founder of the Findhorn "new age" community in Scotland, and several charismatic leaders and their communities. We also interviewed a young couple we ran into quite unexpectedly who could not be called mature spiritual leaders, but whose way and view of life expressed a quality of holiness that called us to further probing. We also included a researcher in the area of "stages" of faith development.

Before discussing the themes of harmony and contrast which emerged from these interviews, it would be helpful to turn to the following page and scan the list of people with whom we talked.

Interviewees

Ruth Barnhouse, psychiatrist, Cambridge, Mass.
Eileen and Peter Caddy, Findhorn Community, Scotland
John Callahan, Teresa and others, Madonna House, Canada
William Connolly, S.J., Center for Religious Development, Cambridge, Mass.
Verna Dozier, Episcopal Diocese of Washington, D.C.
Mark Dyer, Episcopal Diocese of Massachusetts
James Forbes, Union Theological Seminary, N.Y.
Donald Foree, S.J., El Retiro Jesuit Retreat Center, Calif.
James Fowler, Emory University, Atlanta
David Gaerets, S.T.B., Benedictine Abbey, Pecos, N.M.
Maria Jose Hobday, O.S.F., Popago Indian Reservation, Sells, Ariz.
Hans Hofmann, University of Massachusetts, Boston
Conrad Hoover, Church of the Saviour, Washington, D.C.
Alan Jones, General Theological Seminary, N.Y.

Lawrence Kushner, Congregation Beth El of Sudbury, Mass.
George MacLeod, Iona Community, Scotland
Ted and Donna Motsinger, Taos, N.M.
Basil Pennington, O.C.S.O., St. Joseph's Abbey, Mass.
Stephen Plummer, Good Shepherd Mission, Ariz.
A group of Navajo Episcopal laity, Farmington, N.M.
Graham Pulkingham, Community of Celebration, Scotland
Tarthang Tulku Rinpoche, Nyingma Institute, Berkeley
Linda and Peter Sabbath, Thomas Merton Center, Quebec
Billy Sam, Navajo Medicine Man, Ariz.
Seung Sahn Soen-Sa, Providence Zen Center, R.I.
William Sheehan, O.M.I., Oblate College, Washington, D.C.
+Edward McCorkell, O.C.S.O., Our Lady of the Holy Cross
    Monastery, Berryville, Va.
Stephen Usinowicz, O.C.S.O., Our Lady of the Holy Cross Monastery,
    Berryville, Va.
Howard Thurman, Howard Thurman Educational Trust, San Francisco
An Anonymous Hermitess

The Interviewing Process

Major credit for the conduct and design of these interviews belongs
to Tilden Edwards who designed the questions and conducted most of
the interviews himself. He also accomplished the difficult task of pulling
the results of the interviews into a meaningful format for this chapter.
Dolores Leckey, Henry Atkins and Barry Evans also helped conduct
some of the interviews.

At the outset we felt that the most meaningful results would be
achieved if we could establish some consistent line of questioning for all
the interviews, so that afterwards we would be able to compare and
contrast responses to specific questions. But as might be expected, it
became very difficult to frame questions "about" spiritual development
and contemplative practice which would be open enough to allow for the
wordless quality of the truth we were attempting to discover. This
problem was identical to that which we encountered throughout this
study: how can one learn, think, talk and write "about" a truth which is
altogether beyond words?

The best resolution we could find for this problem was to list a set of
questions which could be used as guidelines for the interviews, but
which we would not expect to be asked verbatim. In other words, we
established the *areas* we wanted to ask about, and then asked about

them in the best way possible at the time. Our list consisted of 10 basic areas:

    1. What are your assumptions about the *intent* and *process* of spiritual formation? In other words, what do you think it is for, and how do you think it happens?
    2. How do you understand the relationship of freedom and grace? In other words, what is the role of the individual person's will and intentionality in spiritual growth?
    3. How do you understand intent and method in spiritual direction and friendship? This area was designed to clarify the interviewee's perceptions of leadership roles and methods.
    4. What (if anything) is "inadequate" in past understandings of spiritual formation? In other words, what do you feel we can learn from modern or different approaches such as behavioral science, differing religious traditions, etc.?
    5. What is the place of non-solitude experience in spiritual awareness? In other words, how important is community and relationships with others?
    6. What is the value of going deep in one tradition with commitment as compared to a more eclectic approach?
    7. Do you feel there is one path within a given tradition, or many of equal value in moving toward union with God?
    8. What are the primary needs of your church or religious base in today's world?
    9. Whom do you most respect as "spiritually realized" persons today and in the past?
    10. What do you affirm or question in what we are doing in Shalem? This was our way of asking for specific critique of our approaches.

As indicated, these questions were seldom asked in just the way they are worded here. In general, they simply represented guidelines for the course we wanted the interviews to follow. We hoped that this more open approach would allow enough space for the varieties of people and situations we would encounter, and avoid too much stifling of the intuitive and numinous qualities we would be trying to explore.

In large part, we feel we were successful with this, but it is of course impossible to maintain a full openness to the truth when one is operating under even the vague restrictions imposed by the structure of our questions. Thankfully, neither the truth itself nor the interviewees can be made to conform to a stable conceptual structure. A delightful example of this occurred while Tilden was attempting to "interview" Korean Zen Master Soen-Sa Nim. To begin with, there was some difficulty with the language, but in spite of this, Tilden experienced the discomfiting sensation that Soen-Sa Nim understood only too well. Suddenly it seemed rather absurd to be trying to ask this man "What are your assumptions about the intent and process of spiritual formation?" One had the feeling that Soen-Sa Nim probably didn't have any assumptions about anything.

So Tilden struggled to find a way of asking how Soen-Sa Nim saw the purpose of spiritual practice. He came up with what sounds like an excellent approach: He simply asked the Zen Master, "Why Zen Meditation?" To which Soen-Sa Nim responded, "Why you want to know, 'why Zen meditation?' "

The direction of conversation rapidly changed into a discussion of confidence. Why would anyone who was confident in his own practice be asking questions about the purpose of that practice? Soen-Sa Nim had cut through the words and questions with incredible speed, and had uncovered the basic reason for our entire study . . . the question of confidence in our own practice. Even at this writing, months after the interview took place, we are still trying to explain to Soen-Sa Nim what "spiritual development" is. And wondering whether we're not just spouting so many words which cloud the truth.

So it is not only the mind-set of our questions which may cloud the truth, but also the verbiage of our answers. Doubtless this will be reflected as we try to present here the themes which have emerged from these interviews. An even deeper limitation is that the words and the experience of the interviews could never substitute for what we might have learned by living with these people through their daily routines and encounters. As C. S. Lewis once said, "Truth is too precise for words."

Assumptions Concerning the Intent and Process
of
Spiritual Formation

The majority of interviewees seemed to share a common underlying intuition that spiritual formation points toward a personal realization in God which is marked by love and by open waiting and desiring God's true image to emerge through each person. This involves relativizing one's conscious sense of self to its deeper, spacious source in God, losing false images and attachments, allowing Divine Life to be shared intimately and spread to others.

The two Buddhist masters did not use the term "God." One spoke of the need not to be attached to the names and forms of Christ or God, except in the early stages of spiritual development. He spoke of those Christians who didn't seem to believe in God but instead in words *about* God. Despite their difference in vocabulary, we sensed that the Buddhists' general view of intent overlapped significantly with the underlying experience of most others. This was especially true as regards clear awareness, nonattachment to "my," and compassion.

Some other divergent or especially poignant responses are seen in these quotations:

1. Sister Maria Jose Hobday's spontaneous answer concerning intent included: "To meet and embrace *all* of life, not choosing this or that, and not falling apart from the pain and tension. From that experience you are able to love everyone more . . . Realizing that *all* of life makes sense or none of it does. Realizing that the Spirit in your own heart is the guru, and God, Jesus, has been present all along. When you die you live. When you think you "have it," you don't. You don't 'hold it' at all."

2. Father Stephen Plummer, a Navajo Episcopal priest, and the Navajo medicine man Billy Sam, indicated that "harmony with nature" was the primary contribution of Navajo spirituality. The "nature" was meant to include other human beings. Teresa, a member of Madonna House, a Christian community which lives with extreme ecological carefulness, came closest to this Navajo understanding when she spoke of entering into obedience to God's plan of loving harmony in all things. This, she said, is "living Christ."

3. George MacLeod, founder of the Iona Community, paraphrasing from James 1:27, said "Pure religion undefiled is to care for the fatherless and widow and keep yourself unspotted from the world: piety (prayer) and politics; total obedience."

4. Peter Caddy, co-founder of the Findhorn Community, spoke of intent as "Spiritualizing matter, materializing spirit, bringing the Kingdom of Heaven on earth, the perfection of man; seeing spirit on all levels, bringing about a change of consciousness toward a wholistic view of life, linking centers of light with the goal of transformation of the planet."

5. Rabbi Lawrence Kushner said the intention is to "see, know, and understand the ultimate nature of reality."

The basic PROCESS of spiritual development also seemed to be similarly understood by a majority of interviewees, even though the specific methods and stages mentioned varied widely.

Most saw the process as involving a thirst for God's presence, attentiveness to grace in one's daily life, labor and birth pains, time alone and with others, prayer and work for others, and an increasing centeredness in the "Big I" of God rather than the little "ego-I."

Most interviewees tended to be somewhat suspicious of any scheme of precise, consistent *stages* of development through which people go. Underlying this suspiciousness was a sense of the subtle, unique development of each individual and an awareness that all important developments happen by grace, for which any conscious process can only be a preparation.

"A person is all over the place at the same time [the only guideline is] dying to our superficial selves in a context of love." (Basil Pennington)

"We have different attachments at different times. We have to let God shatter our idols one by one. Be faithful to where we are, trusting that God will bring to light whatever is hindering the work of the Holy Spirit within us." (The Hermitess)

"Stages are only seen as 'after thoughts.' " (James Forbes)

"Stages exist but you may take three steps forward and then go back four, or you may stay in one place for a long time; moments of presence that produce peace are scattered throughout the stages." (Mark Dyer)

"It is not so much a matter of stages as of states entered and left; these states are not plateaus but elevators—they operate in both directions all of the time, for everybody." (Lawrence Kushner)

Some specific stages which were mentioned (in outline) include:
I. *From William Connolly* (Inspired by Ignatius Loyola):
   1. Life realized as a gift of the Creator
   2. Realization of "unfreedom" and the need for Christ as Saviour
   3. Personal response to Jesus in service to others

II. *From Verna Dozier*
   1. Dissatisfaction: Sense of gap between what is and might be
   2. Wistful stage: romantic, belief there is only "one right way"
   3. Tension of acceptance, but not complacency, regarding the realization that the Kingdom is here, but not fully, and what that fullness depends on is God's grace

III. *From Alan Jones*
   1. Dogmatic images
   2. Desert
   3. Restored images, seeing a human being as a product of "nothing plus image"; wholeness and emptiness at the center

IV. *From James Fowler*
   1. Simple
   2. More differentiated
   3. Putting it all back together with a different perspective (related to Paul Ricouer's "first vs. second naivete")

V. *From Graham Pulkingham*
1. Looking for spirituality as a prop; disillusioned people looking for solace; escapist
2. Accepting some belief in an outside Power
3. Spiritual disillusionment; guilt: the most difficult stage
4. More aggression in dealing with experience (more facing into it)

VI. *From Mark Dyer*
Stages Identified in working with Episcopal clergy:
1. Awareness that someone sold me an inadequate package of goods. "Why wasn't I shown spirituality as the center before?"
2. Discipline taken on unique to that person; dying to the idolatry of the Church, and then refinding it in a way that sees God as God of mercy
3. Struggling with obstacles to growth: sin, stubbornness; realization that life is changing and can't go back, yet afraid to go ahead (person needs a supportive community at this stage badly)
4. Pulling back, because it's all too much; longing for the flesh pots of Egypt
5. Awareness that you're just called to be faithful, not successful; the Peace of Christ takes over; commitment to a long-hard pilgrimage, driving you deeper into compassion

Some specific *methods* mentioned as helpful for development included:

1. "Communal loving prayer and work, with occasional one to one guidance and solitary retreats." (Madonna House)
2. "Unceasing breath-prayer to be used while waking and sleeping; spiritualizing sexual energy; heart-to-heart prayer with Christ; liberation from self-love, self-will, tyranny of senses by intensive process of Kenosis (influenced by Near Eastern and Far Eastern practices). Spiritual journal keeping, including examination of conscience, read twice daily by director; daily sacraments and scripture reading; healing of memories." (Linda Sabbath)
3. "Experience of loving relationships, daily examination of conscience, and one to one guidance." (Donald Foree)
4. "On-going relation to a Spiritual Father, charismatic expressions, journal keeping (especially dreams), and communal prayer and caring helping you to 'know the Lord.'" (David Gaerets)
5. "Staying close to the land and to 'plain people' and to simple living; providing experiences for individuals that help them realize their own littleness, and the Spirit guiding us in our hearts." (Maria Jose Hobday)
6. "A series of means, steps, ideas designed to confront you with the

self-deception with which you ordinarily live; a series of premeditated and organized discomforts; things that will wrench us out of step from the herd." (Lawrence Kushner)

7. " 'Lectio Divina': a classical Cistercian process of Scripturally-based reading, meditation, prayer, and contemplation; other more contemporary techniques such as hatha yoga, the Christian 'mantra', etc., have proved helpful." (Edward McCorkell)

In asking interviewees the source of their religious assumptions, we received a wide range of responses, usually involving both first hand experience and the influence of others. Some of these influences included: Past Christian spiritual masters (e.g., Ignatius, Merton, Theresa of Lisieux, John of the Cross, Teresa of Avila, Gregory of Nyssa); Lurianic Kabbalah; a wide range of current spiritual authors and leaders, some publicly known, many more anonymous individuals; scripture (rarely mentioned directly, yet we think assumed by many); family members who expressed a faithful, loving life; early religious training; social sciences; experiencing the family context of many problems; the "collective spiritual unconscious" of my family line; friends; experience of the Black race in America; experience of being raised in the British working class; the land; plain people; poor people; tradition; learning to keep "half blind"; Eastern gurus; faith; interior experiences (including charismatic and reincarnational); community work and experience.

Understanding of the Relationship between Freedom and Grace

Questions in this area pressed interviewees to look more closely at how they understood the process of spiritual development to be happening. The historical dialogue on the relation of freedom and grace is large and touchy; schisms in the church have come about over it. This is perhaps the most subtle and complex area of all those we examined; one for which any conceptual answer seems inadequate and easily misunderstood.

We usually tried to explore the area of freedom and grace by asking one or more specific sub-questions. One of these was "What can a person do to 'grow' spiritually?" The concensus seemed to be that everything important is given. There are disciplines, commitments, and attitudes that can help put us in effective touch with the graceful givens in our lives, but even these and their "results" are in some subtle way a part of grace.

> "The acquisition of skill is merely like the operation of a giant roto-rooter clearing out your channel so that God's grace can flow through it. In the metaphor of each person being a cell in the mystical body of Christ it is useful to take that really literally. You have to do your part and be very active, but you are not the central nervous system—Christ is the head. Each of us must remember that we are only one part of the spiritual ecological system, one piece of the jigsaw puzzle, one actor in a complex drama—the whole is known only to God." (Ruth Barnhouse)

> "Most people don't just stumble into it—where your heart is there is your treasure." (Verna Dozier)

> "We can set the environment, but gift is what comes; all you can do is be faithful. *Sufficient* grace is given to all. An *efficacious* life takes this and allows it to be effective." (Mark Dyer)

> "Life takes you, you don't take it. If you try too hard you will have lost it. However, go for the dangers of life. Once you understand life, discipline is o.k. However, before you understand life, discipline can hinder." (Maria Jose Hobday)

> "You cannot accelerate the process—though you can inhibit it. You can break down barriers, but you can add nothing." (Hans Hofmann)

> "God has got to be present in every moment of spiritual awareness. Sometimes He is present to those who don't work hard. Other times He is silent to those who do work." (Lawrence Kushner)

Another sub-question asked was, "How do you understand the relationship of "spiritual" development to psychological or "ego" development? Answers consistently refused to see any ultimate distinctions here: There is one human development process with various dimensions. The whole process intertwines grace and freedom.

> "There must first be a self [ego] to surrender." (Alan Jones)

> "The ego must develop first—become more ego-centric, let this run its course to overflowing, until the pod is ripe." (Hans Hofmann)

> "Psychology and religion are two ways of approaching the same territory: Each is dealing with reality within." (Conrad Hoover)

> "There is no difference, but human development is *grounded* in my sense of a Creator calling me to fullness of who I am; without this, development would become a technique and not a response." (Verna Dozier)

"Classical Freudian psychoanalysis has parallels through the first week of the Ignatian exercises; Jung has parallels through the second; but there is more, the most important part." (Ruth Barnhouse)

"Spiritual development has the effect of helping one ultimately serve He who is the parent of all egos." (Lawrence Kushner)

A third sub-question asked some interviewees probed the relation between contemplative experience and social discernment and action. Answers pointed toward no ultimate distinction between these dimensions, either. Grace and freedom were seen as operative in each and both were viewed as essential dimensions of spiritual development which need each other. When one is most spiritually mature, social action seems just to "happen," with less conscious "figuring out."

"Discernment and action grow out of quiet time, as out of a deep well." (Verna Dozier)

"You have to be concretely at work in the world as a channel of grace . . . If you're really 'in touch' this will spill over (a spontaneous more than willed process). But I also agree with Thomas Merton who wrote somewhere that this is not essential for hermits who hold the whole cosmos together with their prayer." (Conrad Hoover)

"We need to just be faithful to who we are, and God will give the witness—we don't need to worry about the witness." (Hermitess)

"The spectrum of religious personalities includes those whose motion is outward and those whose motion is inward: the prophet and the mystic. God speaks to both of them; they react in different ways." (Lawrence Kushner)

Responses Regarding Spiritual Direction and Friendship

Since relatively little is in print in this important area, we were particularly concerned to learn from the wide experience of these spiritual leaders. In most interviews we focused on four sub-questions:

How much "SPACE" vs. "STUFF" is important?

Responses were nearly unanimous in giving priority to "space," i.e., to a listening presence, rather than to "stuff," i.e., initiative, content, and substantive direction from the director or friend. Behind this priority lay a number of assumptions shared by most interviewees about the nature of spiritual guidance:

1. Real guidance is from the Holy Spirit or Lord within us:

   "The person is learning the process of the Lord's authority." (William Connolly)

   "The relationship is a triangle with the Holy Spirit working with and through the spiritual director and the individual seeking guidance." (James Forbes)

   "You never truly initiate anything." (Maria Jose Hobday)

   "Direction is to open people to *hear* God, to listen to Christ. The primary intent is setting the heart in God. It is the Holy Spirit who is the real director of souls. The spiritual father or mother is a trusted friend who helps a person discern movements of the Holy Spirit in his/her life. The director should be calling persons to prayer, to deeper union with God and all in Him." (Peter and Linda Sabbath)

2. Each person is unique and at a unique point in his or her spiritual journey:

   "You must respect where a person is; let them make decisions; don't press on them more than is asked; you may take initiative in interpreting the Spirit, but this must resonate with the person: S/he may not be ready." (Basil Pennington)

   "A person's inner sense of integrity should not be violated." (Conrad Hoover)

   "People often have to go through things; it's not my place to disrupt that process; life does not rape, but we do at times." (Hans Hofmann)

   "The director helps carry burden of the one who comes—prays for and with him/her. And he loves the directee and then gives counsel." (Hermitess)

3. The director's intuition is most important in what is done. This can even lead to offering more "stuff" than "space" at times, if this seems called for:

   "What you do depends on the person: People tell you what they need and you respond; sometimes people just want a drink of water." (Maria Jose Hobday)

   "I try to listen and be intuitive." (Conrad Hoover)

   The importance of the director's intuition was more emphasized by the

Korean Zen Master: "If you're not thinking, already you are complete, you have everything. If you are thinking, I cannot help you, but I point to moment to moment keeping the correct situation, that is, 'just like this' is truth." (Seung Sahn Soen Sa)

4. Most interviewees assumed that offering space or stuff in direction is not just a managed psychological method, but an opening to real divine power:

"The director functions as a channel of divine power helping others to open their channel to the divine." (Ruth Barnhouse)

"It is the Spirit who gives life in direction: God's power works through weak human instruments; thus the director need not be a paragon of virtue but rather a compassionate person who binds up wounds and helps his brother carry his burden." (Hermitess)

"The director is a sacrament really transmitting grace." (Stephen Usinowicz)

The kinds of "stuff"—content which could be initiated by the director—mentioned included:

1. "Always work with prayer because the presence of prayer in a person is a sign of the Presence of the Holy Spirit initiating desire for God expressed in petition and fulfilling that inspired petition by a further infusion of gratitude and praise." (Stephen Usinowicz)

2. Confirmation of a person's experiences and directions if they express the "fruits of the Spirit" and direction toward the Lord.

"I often don't know where a person is going, but I help him concentrate on what's happening: whether it is toward or away from the Lord." (William Connolly)

3. Particular methods to help a person be in deeper intuitive touch (e.g., work with mandalas, energy conversion, journal keeping, and breath prayer at the Merton Center).

4. Helping to conceptualize experiences.

5. Suggesting readings.

Since primary direction is seen to come from the Divine within and between persons, it is not surprising that many interviewees were leery of the term "spiritual director." Spiritual friend or father or mother were terms substituted by some. Even those who easily used the term director did not give it connotations of arbitrary authority. Authority rests in the subtle Holy Presence before whom sit both director and directee, seeking discernment and communion.

A few interviewees gave particular weight to the place of the community in guidance. This was most pronounced with Peter Caddy, who placed great emphasis on the growth value of Findhorn's communal living process; the new age we are in, he believes, is marked by communal discernment and not by the individual master, though such a person can have value at a certain stage of development. At the same time, he and Eileen both emphasize the priority of each person listening for God from within.

What are the most important qualifications for a Spiritual director or friend?

Answers to this question reflected overall agreement concerning two key areas of qualifications:

1. Personal spiritual commitment, experience, and knowledge, prayer, and humility.

2. The capacity to be caring, sensitive, open, and flexible with another person, not projecting one's own needs or fostering long-term dependency.

The following fragments of answers bring out special dimensions not obvious in the above. The director or friend needs to:

"Be a theologian, i.e., one who doesn't get trapped by any foreign environment; have a sense of one's own personal and religious institutional history, seeing their pilgrim relativity and the more basic gift of peace." (Mark Dyer)

"Be over 35 years old." (Ruth Barnhouse)

"Have experienced a movement from despair to grace, trust the healingness of the universe, and delight in the freedom of others." (James Forbes)

"Humbly realize that he is an instrument of grace, have a spirit of prayer, common sense, and intelligence." (Donald Foree)

"Stand in a particular tradition, yet be able to translate for those who don't; have a context for ongoing accountability for content and method; have gotten through Messianism . . . everybody needs this." (James Fowler)

"Have an applied knowledge of both psychological and spirituality areas." (Many Interviewees)

"Pray three hours a day in order to be able to discern; hospitality; openness; an ability to welcome all of life." (Maria Jose Hobday)

"Have no expectation or anticipation of where a person should go—not my will but Thine be done; the bee keeper is the most spiritual, least assuming." (Hans Hofmann)

"Have a deep experience of life in all its dimensions." (Conrad Hoover)

"Do oneself out of business." (Alan Jones)

"Have a loving patience." (Edward McCorkell)

"Have the capacity to step aside and let the Spirit of Christ do the direction—skill development is secondary to this." (Peter and Linda Sabbath)

"I one hundred percent believe in my true self, which is the absolute; no subject, no object. The name for this is clear mind. Only the sky is blue, the tree is green." (Seung Sahn Soen Sa)

"Have personal realization and comprehensive confidence." (Tarthang Tulku Rinpoche)

"Have detached compassion, not *needing* the relationship; also, gifts of the Spirit and a radical self-giving to the Lord." (Basil Pennington)

"Be unpossessive, relying on nothing in self, but on poverty in God's mercy." (Stephen Usinowicz)

"Be in full communion with the whole of your own humanity—not airy-fairy; be in the body of some tradition where there can be external validation of your experience." (Graham Pulkingham)

"Be a fellow searcher." (Lawrence Kushner)

"Capacity to notice movement of the Spirit, and to provide an environment out of which person can pay attention and allow this intuitive noticing to become an important part of his/her life." (William Sheehan)

What is the Value of Male-Female Spiritual Relationships?

Most interviewees asked this question affirmed the great potential value of male-female spiritual friendship. A few felt sex made no difference.

Distinctive comments included these:

"A male-female spiritual relationship is ideal, especially for an all male or all female community." (Donald Foree)

"It is disastrous to separate the two . . . a deep, intimate friendship/ affection (non-genital) with the opposite sex is vital." (David Gaerets)

"Male/female spiritual friendship *can* be entered into without fear. It should be tested by its fruits. Does it lead each one closer to God? One test is to ask yourself, can I pray for him or her? Am I at peace when I do?" (Hermitess)

"Whether you choose a man or woman is a very individual matter." (Conrad Hoover)

"Sexual boundaries are not important; but there are some things a woman can understand better about another woman." (Linda and Peter Sabbath)

"It is important to have good cross-sex relationships somewhere, but I'm not sure if this must be in spiritual guidance; perhaps it is best for a man to have a spiritual mother, together with strong male peer relationships." (Basil Pennington)

"Male-female relationships help express the social Trinity of two persons who imitate the Father as source of spiritual gifts, giving to each other in the love of the Holy Spirit, and the Son, by receiving from each other in the love of the same Holy Spirit. In my experience, deep spiritual friendships between any of the sexes is a gift not given to all. Each person has masculine and feminine characteristics. A man and woman through love and spiritual union, help each other to discover these characteristics and integrate them, becoming whole persons." (Stephen Usinowicz)

"For 3,000 years, mind, science, man, West, action have dominated—now is the time when these two polarities need to be balanced within us." (Peter Caddy)

"Light and love, intellect and intuition, heart and mind all need to come into balance within each person and in celibate relationships between men and women." (Eileen Caddy)

How Do You Deal With a Person's Interior Experiences?

Only a few persons were asked this question directly because of its complex nature and because many interviewees covered it indirectly while responding to other questions. Those we did ask had such comments as these:

"I tend to refer them to particular other persons if they seem to be gifted with authentic visions, or to therapists if the experiences seem crazy." (Donald Foree)

"I look for experiences that force those asking to see the fruits of what they're saying; they must sort out the experiences for themselves; I will share what I know." (Maria Jose Hobday)

"Genuine interior experiences flow primarily from the intuitive-spiritual level of a person, resulting in the fruits of the Holy Spirit, such as peace and joy. These experiences can flow over to the intellectual part in the form of word and locutions as well as into the animal part or imagination, resulting in corporeal 'visions.' The director, as a discerner of spirits, focuses his attention on the spiritual fruits, attributing little importance to the overflow." (Stephen Usinowicz)

"I look for the fruits of the Spirit (as in Gal. 5.22 and I Cor. 13); spiritual and drug experiences are not the same thing." (Edward McCorkell)

What Are Your Perceptions of What Seems To Be "Inadequate" in Past Understandings of Spiritual Formation?

This question usually was elaborated as follows: "Is there anything *essential* or *helpful* to learn from science, Eastern religions, political experiments, etc." Most interviewees felt that there is nothing *essentially* new, yet that there are some new developments which are helpful.

One stressed that we simply are in a *different* age, not a better or worse one. Positive new developments centered around three areas:

1. *Human psychological understanding*

"We have a better understanding of anger, fear, and guilt, and a new awareness that a person must be mature in a sense of self-worth before s/he can share His humiliations." (William Connolly)

"We're clear now that there are many other bases of 'sinning' than our old restricted sense of the sinful nature of man; depth psychology is valuable." (David Gaerets and many others by implication)

2. *A more cosmic, dynamic, developmental world view*

"This is a time of cultural stage change, moving toward integration of our 'shadows' and overcoming of our self-righteousness. Current culture has helped us to de-mystify and democratize spirituality." (James Fowler)

"A cosmic leap, a world consciousness is here that the disciples didn't have; also, a rediscovery today of the communal, and leadership rising from the people." (Maria Jose Hobday)

"We see the inadequacy of legalism. The Spirit speaks in a multiplicity of ways. In some cases the structures left no room for movement of the Spirit and He was squelched. A person was molded into a form or pattern and his or her gifts, needs, etc., were ignored for the sake of the institution." (Hermitess)

"John of the Cross knew everything, but now we are less rigid and structured: We see that order must be tentative, relative—life does its own ordering." (Hans Hofmann)

"Today there is more a sense of unfolding, development, evolution, e.g., Aquinas thought woman inferior, today we are beyond that." (Stephen Usinowicz)

" 'Revelation is complete with John's Gospel; the rest is working it out,' said John Newman. That 'working out' today finds us in a more lively time of growth in love, unity, communications, and fulfillment of human potential." (Basil Pennington)

"We are in a new age marked by synthesis and planetary consciousness." (Peter Caddy)

"A new Pentecost is coming, with all things in common, where we will live simply that others may simply live." (George MacLeod)

3. *A view of Eastern religions as potentially, but not necessarily helpful in terms of methods and understandings for spiritual awareness*

"Dialogue with others (religious, sciences) helps break open our symbols and images, leading to a cosmic Christianity; only God is Catholic and Christian." (Alan Jones)

"Though Christianity and Buddhism came from somewhat different points of view, they can share much concern with one another. Westerners have a strong sense of social concern and involvement which the Eastern traditions can learn from. And Buddhists have developed methods for attaining higher awareness which could be very helpful to Westerners." (Tarthang Tulku Rinpoche)

Five people felt that our current culture is worse off today than previously in terms of understanding spirituality. Examples of how they see our present culture as being less hospitable to spiritual depth include:

"We have been so absorbed in extracting nature's secrets and establishing psychological distance that there has been no felt need to get in touch with deeper, more profound reality. Adjustment to our new power for discontinuity of the biological process makes for something brand new: complete despair about the future. We are using the energy of the earth to commit suicide: This puts fear in us." (Howard Thurman)

"Science has narrowed and blurred our awareness of the way reality is, so that we are worse off than a fourth century mystic (but science positively has helped us to follow the Creator more closely in creativity)." (James Forbes)

"Compulsory education is a problem today for the natural development of the mystical life." (Peter and Linda Sabbath)

"There seems to have been a greater spiritual/psychological integration in *past* spiritual masters than today, as in William of Thierry." (Edward McCorkell)

"Though much technology has been developed during this century, often people do not know how to use it. We have collected much information and have developed certain levels of consciousness, but genuine awareness is much vaster than knowledge, or what we call consciousness. Unless we learn to contact this deeper level of awareness, then our attempts to improve the world's external situation may only lead to further imbalance, pollution, and general misfortune. Without awareness, virtuous activity is not possible." (Tarthang Tulku Rinpoche)

What Is the Place of Non-Solitary Experience in Spiritual Awareness?

We did not have occasion to ask specifically about this area in most interviews since it was usually covered by answers to other questions. Interviewees were in general agreement that both solitude and non-solitude experiences form an integral continuum through which spiritual awareness happens. Kushner was an exception: He puts central emphasis on the spiritual context of the praying congregation: "It is paradoxical, there is solitude even in a praying congregation." A majority of interviewees, as it turned out, were living testimonials to the importance of community because they themselves lived or worked in fairly intensive religious communities. In these settings they maintain a rhythm of life characterized by mutual accountability and service with others who share their religious commitment.

What Is the Value of Committing Oneself to One Tradition vs. A More Eclectic Involvement?

There was general agreement that it is essential to go deeply into one tradition. Many saw this depth in a paradoxical way: The further "in" you go in one tradition the more it opens one to understanding and respecting those who have gone deeply into other traditions. Most interviewees supported the potential value of learning from the ways of other deep traditions, as long as this was done from the vantage-point of ongoing identity with one's own tradition. A major exception to this focus on tradition was Peter and Eileen Caddy and the Findhorn community in general, which sees us in a new age of synthesis that brings to fulfillment and oneness all religious traditions. Peter Caddy said that one can move from one path to another like stepping stones, but you reach a point where you must experience the birth of Christ within, and move into a more universal path.

"Commitment, roots somewhere is very important, without this there is no accountability. Only then can you reach out to other traditions." (Verna Dozier)

"People not associated with a religious tradition are parasites. They live off the efforts of others who have struggled with the paradox of a tradition." (Ruth Barnhouse)

"We need to explore other traditions in relation to our own, and beyond this realize that God is not limited to history as it has been. I do not mean indifference to one's own commitment but openness to a variety of traditions thereby deepening one's own; it is our tradition to be shocked by the workings of God." (Donald Foree)

"You can only depart from a tradition if you live it; if you want a person to be a good Zen student in the West, he had better have been a good Christian or Jew. When you go to the bottom of the tradition, you meet everyone else. To be secure frees you to search. Take Jesus at his most profound; look for the fruits: If they show up in Buddhism take a look at what is going on." (Maria Jose Hobday)

"You must start from somewhere. The past has to tell its story before you can let it go. Otherwise, it remains a shadow over you. Studying theology is a necessary emptying. Disciplined commitment is necessary." (Hans Hofmann)

"The Spirit is in history not just in the Church." (Graham Pulkingham)

"One's tradition is the matrix, the grid on which to arrange the spiritual data that comes in. You can't borrow someone else's grid without a major change in your universe. However, the grids are pretty much similar." (Lawrence Kushner)

"You're of little worth to yourself, others, or God unless you are rooted somewhere." (Conrad Hoover)

"You shouldn't go into contemplation with an empty stomach. Liturgy and Word are proper food for facing the imageless." (Alan Jones)

Soen Sa-Nim told a story that seems to support "going in" one way, yet to the same end: "In Japan I went to the baths. One door was marked 'men,' the other, 'women.' I went into the men's door and found women in there. Back outside, I thought there must be some misunderstanding of terms. Perhaps in this country, they reverse the words. So I went into the door marked 'women.' There were women there, too. Both doors opened into the very same place." (Sueng Sahn Soen-Sa)

The Navajos interviewed were in a different situation: a struggle for cultural survival in the larger, pressing-in Western culture. Even for the active Christians it was very important to integrate Navajo legends, symbols, and practices into their religious practice. In fact, one Christian said that the Church was the best institutional hope for helping preserve Navajo culture. Stephen Plummer felt that Navajo spirituality's biggest contribution to Christians is harmony with nature, while the Church offers one God, worship, Jesus, and preaching.

Is There One Path, or Many of Equal Value in Moving Toward Union with God?

This question is focused not on different traditions, but on different ways *within* a tradition, e.g., contemplation, theological knowledge, charismatic experience, moral action. On the whole, participants would have changed "of equal value" to "of *complementary* value," and support the rightness of different paths for different people at different points in their lives. However, most interviewees believed that some form of contemplative path is essential at some point.

"Contemplative (as distinct from monastic) life is discovering your true self in God: This is essential for every person. By his very being man is made for contemplation." (Edward McCorkell)

"No path should be absolutized." (Verna Dozier)

"There are many paths. The Lord has a thousand ways. Charismatic experience is particularly important to foster today (in the context of sacramental and community life)." (David Gaerets)

"A desert experience of some kind in my experience is a necessary part of the spiritual development process." (Hermitess)

"The contemplative is at the heart of all the traditions. The parents who have done the most are those who have taught their children to contemplate all of life. You have to be willing to enter into all worlds: You have to walk in the animal world to understand instinct; you have to be able to relate to women to be a man, etc. You come back into your own world with greater understanding." (Maria Jose Hobday)

"Some people have a spiritual problem that they don't want to face; so they stick with a system long enough to get to that problem point but then they leave and start over again in another system. Using the image of a mountain: Such people do not climb; when the going gets tough they move around to a different starting point near the base of the mountain. This does not get them any nearer to the top. But those who tackle their problems on the path which they have started do go up; here there is genuine fellowship because they are closer to others who are on the same journey even if they have come up a different side of the mountain. We need to pay attention to personality types: Different people may need different paths." (Ruth Barnhouse)

"All need liberation from the drives of survival, security, and significance. If you 'seek first the Kingdom' you will see the complementarity of life. All need to re-integrate their experience with everyday reality." (James Fowler)

What Are the Primary Needs of the Church Today?

Answers tended to converge in three areas:

1. *The Church needs to be more of a sub-culture*, obedient to the radical calling of its tradition. It needs to resist identification with those societal values which narrow, oppress, and domesticate, and it needs to cleanse itself of its own institutionalized forms of these sins.

   "The Church needs death. It increasingly is in the state of the synagogue at the time of Jesus: over-organized, over-concerned with ritual; it needs a fresh wind of the Spirit, permanent openness." (Verna Dozier)

   "It needs to counter current relativism, where the norms lead you to hide any sense of truth and right." (James Fowler)

   "Civic religion has gotten in the way of understanding the Church's serious historical identity." (Mark Dyer)

   "You have to be able to feel, think, touch the earth, (etc.); you have to be alert to be integrated. Our society dulls. The call is simplicity. The

Church has to be something of a lunatic fringe to be gospel true. It needs to be plain, at home with the poor to promote deinstitutionalization." (Maria Jose Hobday)

"The Church needs to be a thorn in society's flesh. It is the only thing in society that does this. It says, 'Yeh, but . . .' But trouble occurs when it says, 'I am it'; the institution is a toolshed." (Hans Hofmann)

"It needs to get out of the prison of its institutional forms and sell-out to capitalism, affluence, oppression, and success, and re-claim simplicity, a dynamic sense of a personal God and obedience to the radical demands of the Gospel." (Conrad Hoover)

"The Church needs to address itself to the timeless rather than the time/space bound needs of people. We have amazing skill in meeting the latter needs, but not the former (timeless) ones." (Howard Thurman)

"The sangha (Buddhist community) is too elitist. It needs to see the uniqueness of persons and pay attention to the social level more." (Tarthang Tulku Rinpoche)

2. At the same time, *the Church needs to serve the real needs of the people more fully*: The need for justice, for broad spiritual insight, commitment, growth, and fulfillment.

3. Many interviewees also pointed to the need to *re-find and respect the mystery of life and faith*:

"The Church should not interpret the Master's intuition with inflexible words about it." (William Connolly)

"The 'Rabbi' is a good metaphor today: always walking, teaching, telling stories; using the Socratic method, setting the environment; never trapped by a foreign environment." (Mark Dyer)

"The Church needs mystery—we must be willing to know things without being able to justify or explain this knowledge from a rational point of view. The mystery can be compared to a stained glass mobile hanging in a doorway—it will never look twice the same and yet its identity endures. We must be willing to contemplate it and share our varying insights into it. Too often, instead, we rush in and photograph it, and then go into another room to argue with each other about whose photograph is correct!" (Ruth Barnhouse)

"The Church needs a renewed vision of its task, and to relate the reality of Christ to the world of creation and vice-versa." (Graham Pulkingham)

"It needs to turn within and realize that the Presence of God is there to guide us directly." (Peter Caddy)

"It needs openness, freedom, joy." (Eileen Caddy)

"The Church needs a recovery of the feast of the Transfiguration, when Jesus was at-one-ment between the spiritual and material. It needs to realize that the whole material order is the Body of Christ, and the Final Coming will be the fulfillment." (George McLeod)

On the whole, participants seemed to be in ongoing tension with the institutional expressions of their traditions, living within them, yet as a kind of "loyal opposition."

Who Do You Most Respect as "Spiritually Realized" Persons Today and in the Past?

Many interviewees seemed to have a hard time coming up with names in response to this question, particularly in terms of living people. Extremely few living *public* figures were mentioned. This does not seem to be a time of outstanding public spiritual leaders. Those few mentioned more than once included Mother Teresa of Calcutta, Henri Nouwen, and George Maloney of Fordham (all Roman Catholics), but no more than three persons mentioned any one of these.

In terms of the recent past, Thomas Merton and Martin Luther King were mentioned more than once, but again by only a very few.

Most living or recently living persons mentioned were little known priests, sisters, bishops, hermits, monks, teachers, and lay people, including parents (particularly the Navajos), with whom participants had very personal and powerful contact at some point in their lives.

Howard Thurman had a poignant story of a barely literate old woman in his congregation who influenced him strongly by her silent expressions as he preached. She came to church with a deep sense of calling to help him in this way. Such unexpected help fit Thurman's sense that "a spiritual leader is one to whom that title scarcely occurs. God scatters Himself in many people and decides under what circumstances and people He will emerge."

James Forbes pressed this to a universal calling when he said, "In God's scheme, each one of us is used toward consummation in Him."

Peter Caddy spoke in terms of spiritually advanced *communities* as well as individuals, believing that different ones manifest different strengths.

In terms of those respected from the past, again there were no names mentioned by more than two or three people. These included John of the Cross, Teresa of Avila, Francis of Assisi, Theresa of Lisieux, the Buddha, Ignatius Loyola, the early Desert Fathers. Others mentioned tended to be well known Western mystics of past centuries.

Scriptural persons seemed to be assumed rather than explicitly mentioned. Some mentioned Christ specifically. Sister Maria Jose Hobday felt that "Somehow it is only in Jesus that I find the one I can fully admire. It was the lack of show in him. Plain people were attracted to him. People have it in parts, but only Jesus has it all."

A few others also mentioned specific characteristics they respected in certain holy people: "Capacity to live with ambiguity"; "Intense commitment to things of the spirit and works of the world"; "A kenosis piety of spiritual abandonment"; "People who transcend themselves"; "People who care for others, and have courage to pursue their vision of right, even at threat of their own being."

Verna Dozier perhaps spoke for many when she said, "I respect different people at different stages of my life; individuals don't last for me."

Basil Pennington noted the communication that seems to flow between spiritual leaders: "There are many criss-crossed paths of the holy ones." He quoted, "God loves to bring his darlings together."

What Do You AFFIRM and QUESTION in What We Are Doing in Shalem?

This question was asked directly only of those who had some personal knowledge of our work through our writings or explanation. This amounted to about half of the interviewees. However, we did pick up indirect affirmations and critiques from others through their answers to different questions.

On the whole, those interviewed were very affirmative toward Shalem's approach. In general it was sensed that very few resources exist which offer serious, long-term help with contemplative spiritual development, particularly for "everyday" religious leaders and laity. Many felt strongly that contemplation has been restricted to a few "special" monastic people in the popular mind, but that it really belongs to everyone, and needs to be made available more publicly, as Shalem is helping to do.

Some of the more particular aspects of Shalem's work singled out by interviewees for affirmation are these:

"Shalem's way of not pushing people: allowing a slow process, giving them opportunity to see what is good for them, and dealing with their anger at religious structures. Techniques are used to aid personal growth, including interaction with 'spiritual friends,' yet with an awareness (I hope) that the only way a person is going to grow is by his own freedom, not by techniques." (William Connolly)

"Its soberness of scope: Shalem doesn't attempt to do a massive thing. It isolates spiritual development as too important to 'just happen,' and gives a variety of ways to get at it." (James Forbes)

"Anything that will quiet mind and body is good. Eastern approaches are helpful in their ways of showing distinctions between intellectual and experiential pursuits." (Hermitess)

"Shalem's loose organization is important: The more you get organized the more trouble will come. It needs to keep moving, be honest, straightforward." (Hans Hofmann)

"The structure of the long-term groups is good, including hatha yoga, and sharing experiences and questions as a way of shared spiritual direction. Also, the encouragement of a rhythm of daily individual solitude and group prayer." (Edward McCorkell)

"I like its primary thrust toward church leaders: going where the church is, and beginning where people are." (Basil Pennington)

"Journal keeping is good: It gives intellect its due, helping to sift experiences and integrate different dimensions of the self without too much analysis. Yet it is kept in the context of deeper, imageless, intuitive contemplative experience." (Stephen Usinowicz)

Questions and concerns about Shalem's work were varied, as the range of quotations below indicates. There was no overall pattern. A few overlapped in worrying that Shalem may offer people too much and not settle them down rapidly enough into one way. A few others worried whether or not we fostered a central enough relation to Christ and Christian tradition or to community responsibility. At the same time, others focused on the dangers of becoming too settled or organized. No one seemed to feel Shalem had "fallen over the line" into these errors, but that these were dangers we needed to watch out for. One person not familiar with Shalem questioned the value of any kind of special spiritual formation group.

"Have long term groups come into a position of identity as a trans-historical people of God, seeing grace and not just exemplars and sociological process in history? Is there enough theological reflection in the sense of 'faith seeking understanding'?" (Mark Dyer)

"Shalem has made an effort to be broadly pluralistic, but hasn't achieved this. The pattern remains pretty much particularistic: contemplative spirituality. Maybe it is best to be particularistic in order to provide depth instead of trying to be more pluralistic internally, and at the same time have dialogue and linkages with others who are different, who can give a critique of Shalem's adequacy. Maybe a journal of comparative spirituality needs to be developed." (James Forbes)

"A primary community with goods held in common is ideal, though not everyone is prepared for this. There should be *houses* of formation rather than *schools* of formation, wherein a lived situation in community can be focused upon." (David Gaerets)

"You should take whatever group you are naturally in and grow with it. Groups created for spiritual search are false. We cannot have as the good of a group spiritual fulfillment. Spiritual growth is given in the process of other stuff, in the most unlikely times and places. Spiritual insight is not a goal. It is just found." (Lawrence Kushner)

"It is good that Shalem is there when people need it. It is weak if it doesn't push them out into the world as they are empowered. If it gets too comfortable, watch it." (Maria Jose Hobday)

"Be sensitive to your freedom to pull out, to outgrow. We would love to stay in the womb. If you are drunk with expansion or contraction, you may not hear the Spirit. How can you pull off something like Shalem in the institutional church? Can old wineskins hold the new wine?" (Hans Hofmann)

"Don't become focused on accountability to foundations, but to the individuals with whom you work." (Conrad Hoover)

"Don't overweight journal keeping: Too much self-analysis can divert a person to self-contemplation, narcissism. Journals are o.k. if the intent is to foster fruits of the Spirit." (Edward McCorkell)

"Are participants able to serve after they've gotten in touch with their spiritual experience? People need healing first, then a service orientation." (William Connolly)

"Be slow to pull people out of a particular way. Begin by opening people to relation with Christ, then they will move better, deeper with other things. You rightfully let talking be secondary. Young people in particular are not hung up on concepts. Yet there is danger if no frame of reference is given. Remember that the rhythm with solitude is different for each person. Don't let people get settled; constantly call them forth: People need encouragement for this, tell them to go home and teach others what they've learned. Cast the seed, the result is God's business. Pass it on, and go on to something else." (Basil Pennington)

Summary

All in all, we were both encouraged and stimulated by our experiences with these interviews. A number of our own assumptions were borne out and supported by those we interviewed. In other cases, the interviews pressed us to deeper clarification and critique of our approaches.

Perhaps the most striking element of all these responses, at least to me, harkens back to that very important second area of questioning; the relation between freedom and grace. While there are many suggestions as to how to go about the business of spiritual "leadership" with groups and individuals, many ways to do it, many attitudes to have towards it and many understandings of precisely what is happening, it seems that in the last analysis it is the work of the Divine rather than that of our own ego-oriented selves which is taking place. It is all within the realm of this Holy Will that our own intentional action takes place. Somehow we must continue to struggle to find the "right" ways, and to do a "good" job, but we can take great heart and find deep confidence that all of our struggles occur within the circle of God's arms. Perhaps if one ever "arrives" at that degree of spiritual maturity where the name, form and image of God is replaced by purely being-with-God, one will no longer need that kind of confidence. But as long as we still feel like individuals who are ministering to other individuals, and as long as our own egos continue to create problems for us to solve and complexities for us to simplify, this faith will remain the source of our energy and the direction for our efforts.

In this context it is with the deepest of gratitude that we can learn from people such as these who are more experienced than we. And it is with similar gratitude that we can pass their understandings, as well as our own, along to others. All of us, the leaders and the students, the experienced and the beginners, are fellow pilgrims on this wonderful trip home. And it makes very good sense that we should help each other as best we can along the way.

13

Questions and Cautions
-A Critique of Our Approach

It hardly needs to be said that the beginning of spiritual development groups is not something which should be undertaken lightly. There are too many dangers and deep human needs involved. The stakes, which deal with the very meaning of human lives, are too high for a casual or flippant approach.

In order to provide ourselves with as much attentiveness to this as possible, we in Shalem have asked for open comment and critique from many sources over the years. We have tried to include people from a variety of traditions on our steering committee and as consultants or advisors. We have regularly asked our participants for feedback and follow-up, prayed for guidance, and questioned each other forthrightly.

The study which resulted in this book was a part of this critical process. Through it, we have been able to clarify more precisely what it is that we have been doing, and how well we have been doing it. In the course of the study we interviewed numerous spiritual leaders, examined data from our own experience, and finally subjected our work to the scrutiny of others through a national conference focused on the manuscript of this book*. We also asked Urban Holmes, the Dean of St. Luke's School of Theology and Vincent Cushing, the President of the

---

*See list of conference participants at the end of this chapter.

Washington Theological Union to write specific theological critique papers on our work.

Virtually everyone who was asked to comment has been very supportive, affirming and encouraging. Vincent Cushing voiced the general response in these words: ". . . I can understand the quiet urgency that has seized the participants in Shalem and on a level of my being far beyond person, history and function I both resonate and appreciate the 'intuitional rightness' of your journey."

Nearly all our consultants agree that Western culture is crying out for deeper spiritual nourishment, and that our approach is a legitimate way of attending to an element of religious life which has been sorely neglected and which somehow must be preserved and cared for. A few have seen our methodology as somewhat immature and superficial. Many have raised concerns about various aspects of our approach. But all have dealt with our work honestly and respectfully, and we can only give them our heartfelt appreciation for their criticism and support.

Apophatic vs. Kataphatic Spirituality

As might be expected, in asking for critique from a large number of people representing a variety of traditions, we have occasionally been met with widely divergent responses. This is illustrated especially well in the dialogue between apophatic and kataphatic spirituality.

Urban Holmes, in his theological critique, pointed out that our approach to spirituality has developed primarily into an *apophatic* form, which assumes that man is incapable of forming an accurate image or conceptualization of God, and that whatever images are formed are usually misleading and may in fact become idolatrous. Thus it seems we sometimes tend to devalue the images, symbols, visions and other phenomena which occur in the course of contemplative practice.

This is contrasted with a *kataphatic* approach to spirituality, in which images and symbols are relied upon as necessary intermediaries to the experience of God. Holmes points out that though apophatic spirituality has very legitimate roots in Christian history, (St. Gregory of Nyssa, the pseudo-Dionysius, The Cloud of Unknowing, St. John of the Cross, etc.), it may appear quite alien to many modern Christians. This is because what little experience modern Christians have with contemplative prayer is almost always of the kataphatic kind (picturing Jesus in Bible stories, keeping images of God or Christ during prayer, etc.).

What Holmes predicted was verified at our national conference. Some of the conference participants identified easily with our open, imageless approach to silence. In fact there were a few, representing more Eastern traditions, who felt that we were not aggressive enough in the negation of images. But there were others, especially those who represented charismatic and other "active-prayer" traditions, who felt we were doing a real disservice by not being more affirming of images and symbolic experiences.

Everyone seems to agree that God cannot be fully comprehended by human beings, and the images we do have of God are at best inadequate. But there is considerable disagreement as to whether one should see those images as helpful or harmful. A Zen approach might consider such images as symptoms of delusion, obstacles to be cast out forthrightly. A charismatic approach would be more likely to see them as gifts from God; revelations in their own right which should be taken quite seriously. Classical Christian mystics have tended to fall in between, seeing images as lower, mediated forms of spiritual experience not to be taken with ultimate seriousness.

The Shalem approach generally lies somewhere in between these two extremes, but there is no question that it has leaned more towards an apophatic attitude (as exemplified by the description of Zen above). In part this arises from our concern that kataphatic spirituality may become idolatrous by making the images and experiences so important that they obscure more than reveal the incomprehensible Truth, Power and Love which lie behind them. But in leaning towards apophatic spirituality, we run the risk of other dangers.

First, there are fewer clear guidelines on the contemplative path for the apophatic pilgrim. Since it is only through images and symbols that specific traditions of faith can be defined, an apophatic approach may at times appear less *specifically* Christian, and the distinctions which delineate Christianity from other faiths may seem blurred. This may be an asset, at least temporarily, for programs which purport to be ecumenical, but it also places additional demands upon participants to keep relating their experiences to their own tradition of faith.

Another potential hazard has to do with one's attitude towards the human condition. In both Judaism and Christianity, there is a long tradition of affirming humanity's broken-ness. The belief here is that since the Garden of Eden it has been given to humankind to struggle with feeling separate from God. Each person has an image of self which separates him or her from the rest of the universe, and we are doomed to live in this state until salvation or redemption occurs. This fallen state is a result of humanity's sinfulness, but it is also a gift from God which makes it possible to see and appreciate our existence, to work towards a better world, and (in Christianity) to be redeemed through Christ. Any approach to spirituality which is true to Christianity or to Judaism must somehow affirm this state of affairs. Unless it is very careful, apophatic spirituality may tend to neglect this affirmation.

Again Zen can be taken as an extreme example of this (though it should be remembered that there are many Zen approaches which are *not* this extreme). In certain Zen schools the human sense of being a separate self is seen as a delusion, a sickness in every sense of the word, and it is fought and derogated by every means possible. Out of this there sometimes grows the assumption that whatever one does in life really isn't worth much until or unless one has achieved enlightenment. When things get to this extreme, one has travelled to a realm which is psychologically idealistic and impractical, culturally unacceptable in the West, and untenable from the standpoint of either Christian or Jewish faith. Vincent Cushing underscored this issue in his critique by pointing out the need for recognizing the "essential incompleteness of the human person."

As Shalem has shown, a moderately apophatic approach to spirituality can help uncover a fresh appreciation of one's faith, but it is important to be cognizant of the dangers involved, and to recognize that an apophatic approach which is too extreme may steer one far away from home.

Sin

A closely related issue is sin. Many of our resource people commented upon the relative absence of any direct confrontation of sin in this book. The word is notably absent, and we have been forced to ask ourselves why. It seems that there are two primary reasons.

First, the consideration of sin requires an in-depth clarification of theology, and this is something Shalem as an organization has only begun to do. We have stressed the importance of our participants' engaging in clarifying their own theology in the light of their individual faiths, but we have minimized and at times actually tried to avoid too much definition of a "Shalem Theology." We are now discovering an increasing need to do this, in such a way as will continue to allow freedom of theological development for our participants.

The second reason for the absence of the word "sin" in much of our writing is a more mundane one. Many of our participants and leaders have had difficulty grappling with the concept of sin. On the one hand many have experienced the somewhat childish "baggage" of sin as "doing bad things" which is loaded with emotional rebellion and distaste. On the other hand, there is the more conceptual understanding of sin as being separate, having travelled away from God, or of trying to be God in mastering one's life. The territory between these two images of sin is a rough one, and it is made increasingly difficult when one is forced by contemplative experience to question one's own dualistic images of good and evil. Because of these difficulties, there is too often a tendency to want to avoid the issue altogether, and this is a real mistake.

Shalem groups have on many occasions tried to address the topic of sin. We have done this with specific experiential explorations of confession, forgiveness, and healing. But it has not been an easy business. A deep encounter with one's sinfulness is not something beginners do well, and in a number of ways we are still very much beginners. It may be too much to expect that beginning group members be able to tackle sin in a mature way. But this is no justification for neglecting the issue. Sooner or later one must confront sinfulness and, if one's path is to remain legitimate, sinfulness must remain a constant companion on one's journey.

Our recommendation, for ourselves and for those who read this book, is to maintain an attentiveness to sin, however it may be conceptualized or felt, regardless of how distasteful or difficult it may be to do so.

Theology

As stated above, in its emphasis on helping individuals clarify their own theological stances, Shalem as an institution has been slow in clarifying its own. The process of this study has helped us begin to make headway in this area.

It is perhaps necessary that a beginning program such as ours must take time in clarifying its theological position. To define too early, or to over-define, may result in an excessively limiting orthodoxy and attachment to superficial interpretations. But to define too casually or not at all may result in a secularized, psychologized hodgepodge which must eventually fall in upon itself. Urban Holmes spoke to this point in his critique when he indicated that he is skeptical about the claims of persons who insist they have no interest in theology. "We all image, even if it is to talk about the lack of images, and that is theology."

So again we recommend for others as well as for ourselves that as programs emerge, their theological implications and directions must be explored and examined carefully. As with sin, this process will often be very difficult and must evolve over time. And probably it cannot be done alone. It has been through the perspectives of others who have looked at our work "from the outside" that we have been able to make the most progress in this area, and we recommend that other programs also avail themselves of external evaluations and critiques. History has shown repeatedly that theological clarification comes more from differences than from consensus.

Community

Some people who read this manuscript without being familiar with Shalem's actual work have come away with the impression that Shalem has tried to be a spiritual community. This is presumably a result of some fuzziness in the writing. We have not seen Shalem as a spiritual community in and of itself, but rather as a vehicle through which individuals uncover fresh ways into the pre-existing communities within their own traditions. It is important to keep this clear, for there is much in community that is not in Shalem, and the learnings and recommendations in this book should not be taken as by any means sufficient for the establishment of spiritual communities.

Spiritual communities need far clearer orthodoxies of faith than Shalem has developed. They require much more long-range follow-up concerning continued growth of their members. And they need much more firm processes of commitment.

There are elements of community within the Shalem experience, but these are useful only as they help individuals grow into resonance with their own communities. As indicated many times before, Pilgrimage Home is not a one-way trip. One must always be careful not to confuse the vehicle one uses with the path one travels or the destination one seeks.

Psychology

Several areas of question have been raised concerning our approach to the spirituality/psychology relationship. First, as might be suspected from the discussion of apophatic and kataphatic spirituality, there are two basic responses to our vision of ego and self-image. On the one hand there are those who feel we have been too supportive of individual ego, too ready to respond to "psychological" needs by providing emotional support and by focusing too heavily on introspection. On the other hand, there are some who would say we have not sufficiently affirmed the existence of self-image and personal ego. Here the issue is that for God to be seen as "other" and worshipped appropriately, there must be a strong sense of "self."

Again this points up an East/West contrast, in which the sense of personal self is respectively either derogated or affirmed. And again, we have chosen a somewhat middle-of-the-road stance which may seem vague or even wishy-washy to critics who represent one end or the other of the spectrum.

My sense is that this moderate stance is neither a cop-out nor an attempt to satisfy everyone by watering down the issue, but rather arises from a recognition that the question of self-image can never be resolved in either/or terms. Human experience is really a both/and situation. For example, every human being has had experiences of oneness where self-image disappears and personal ego seems to merge with an infinite consciousness. Such experiences become more common, or at least more recognizable, in the course of contemplative practice. Almost invariably these unitive experiences are accompanied by a sense of absolute truth. One is left with the feeling of having experienced things *as they absolutely are*.

One natural outgrowth of such experiences is a tendency to reso- nate with more "Eastern" attitudes towards spirituality which pose that images of self are delusory, that images of others are also delusory, and that the only true experience of life is that of egolessness. Here also one finds resonance with certain apophatic Christian mystical approaches in which the goal is recognition of union *with* God rather than relation of self *to* God. And it is here that "dying to be reborn" and "losing oneself to find oneself" assume special mystical meaning.

But this is only one side of human experience. The other side, with much stronger roots in Christian and Jewish history, is the fact that most of the time human beings experience themselves in a dualistic way. Most of the time we *do* experience ourselves as separate, and most of the time we *are* conscious of images of self and other, and we maintain some sense of personal ego autonomy. And whenever we feel this way, we hunger for a closer sense of relationship between ourselves and God.

Christ's messages seem to address this predicament very directly, and it often seems that Christ Himself represents a response to the human balance between union and separation. My sense, therefore, is that an open vehicle for pilgrimage which can allow for the growth of a variety of human beings must somehow acknowledge *both* the delusory nature *and* the sacred giftedness of self-image.

At the close of our national conference, Sandra Schneiders ad- dressed this point beautifully in her discussion of the relationship be- tween East and West. She posed that the challenge raised to Christianity by the East is that of greater physical integration and daring speculative- ness in religion, and that the challenge raised to the East by Christianity is that of exploring the beauty and truth of polarity and duality, and the gratuity of salvation in this regard.

It seems to me that the resolution of this dilemma, if there is to be one, must be acknowledged as ultimately coming from God rather than through the efforts of the individual autonomous ego. In other words, it remains a mystery.

Another question which has been raised regarding our approach is one which seems to surface in nearly every discussion of psychology and spirituality; namely, is it necessary for a person to have a solid sense of identity *before* spiritual growth can occur in a mature or healthy way?

Most modern authorities would say yes. Most people feel that some degree of personal psychological maturity or "ego strength" is a prerequisite for healthy spiritual growth. A frequently heard comment is "You have to *have* an ego before you can give it up." What this means in practice is that certain psychological weaknesses or immaturities may have to be resolved before active spiritual practice can be undertaken effectively, and that spiritual practice is in and of itself no remedy for psychological troubles.

While there seems to be considerable consensus about this point among the authorities we've encountered, I personally have some doubts. For one thing, it is a little too pat. It seems rather arbitrary to place spiritual growth on a hierarchy above psychological growth, and to see psychological maturation as a prerequisite for spiritual maturation. Second, I have met a number of people in my life who would clearly have been diagnosed as psychologically immature, emotionally unstable, highly neurotic or even schizophrenic who, at least in my opinion, radiated spiritual light and guidance in ways far greater and more penetrating than my other "mature" or "normal" acquaintances could even dream of.

The question is an important one, but it will not be resolved here. After all, our judgments as to who is or is not psychologically or spiritually mature are just that—our judgments. And we are not now nor will we ever be the ultimate judges.

This brings us back to another question which has been raised in critiques of our work: the issue of distinguishing between psychology and spirituality. In this book I have attempted to make a case that psychology and spirituality are simply different ways of thinking about the same reality. Many of the people who read the manuscript felt that this was a misleading oversimplification of matters. Some maintained that there are indeed two distinct parts to human consciousness; namely spirit and psyche, and that each has to be addressed in its own right.

Other people maintained a more wholistic perspective on the

human person but still felt it misleading to lump spirituality and psychology together to the extent I have. They would prefer to see the two as separate *aspects* of each human existence, perhaps growing from a basic unity but still very different and very much in need of separate attention. Urban Holmes made a strong case along these lines, indicating that one of the real dangers in blurring the distinctions between psychology and spirituality is that of secularizing one's approach to spirituality. I have no quarrel with this concept, and in fact feel it is more workable and less esoteric than is my formulation in the text.

Methodology

Finally, some questions have been raised about the specific techniques and approaches we've used in our work. Most critics have agreed that a "cafeteria" or "smorgasbord" of varying contemplative methods is helpful in a program such as ours which attempts to respond to the needs of a variety of participants. Some, however, felt that there was so much variety in our program that it might prove confusing or contain too many "alien" approaches for beginners. But others felt that there wasn't *enough* variety; that if we were going to offer a cafeteria we really should cover a wider range of possibilities especially including more from charismatic, Hindu, and other more active or kataphatic traditions.

Nearly everyone agreed that the "cafeteria" approach should be limited to the first year of group work, should be acknowledged as a "beginners' " undertaking, and should give way as soon as possible to greater selectivity and depth within a certain tradition.

Some of our critics cautioned us to be ever more watchful to avoid any preoccupation with technique or any idolatry of "teaching" which could subtly displace the importance of Grace, the Will of God, or the goal of deepening spiritual realization in ongoing life. Similarly, many people suggested an ever more concerted effort to maintain constant integration of spiritual practice with daily life. Some felt that our approach, at least as reflected in this manuscript, did not pay enough attention to daily life, and that in order for an undertaking to be called truly contemplative, it must include every aspect of one's existence.

We in Shalem can only agree with this, and raise it again for those who read this book. It is so very easy for spiritual practice to become idolatrous, whether it does so in terms of technique, teaching, feelings, intellect, images, need-satisfaction, comfort or self importance. One must always be watchful that the means do not eclipse the end, and that the end be as clear and constant as possible.

Too often the simplicity of the goal becomes overshadowed and clouded by the complexity of our struggles towards it. It is not easy, especially when one is trying to establish, evaluate or enrich a program for spiritual growth, to maintain attentiveness to that simple end. Yet, somehow, simplicity is what it is all about. We would do well to keep in our hearts and in the eyes of our minds the Psalmist's phrase with which we began *Pilgrimage Home*:

"BE STILL, AND KNOW THAT I AM GOD"

Participants

Interviewees

Barnhouse, Ruth, Cambridge, Mass.
Dozier, Verna, Washington, D.C.
Forbes, James, Union Theological Seminary, New York
Foree, Donald, S.J., Jesuit Retreat House, Los Altos, Calif.
Hoover, Conrad, Church of the Saviour, Washington, D.C.
Pulkingham, Graham, Community of the Celebration, Scotland
Sabbath, Linda, Thomas Merton Center, Quebec, Canada
Seung Sahn Soen-Sa and interpreters George Bowman and Louise Stanton, Providence Zen Center, R.I.
Sheehan, William, Oblate College, Washington, D.C.

Others

Adams, Jim, St. Mark's Episcopal Church, Washington, D.C.
Allen, Yorke, Rockefeller Bros. Fund, N.Y.
Benignus, Emma Lou, Nat'l. Ministries, Am. Baptist Church, Pa.
Charbeneau, Thomas W., The Center for Comparative Spirituality, Berkeley
Cousins, Ewert, Fordham U., New York, N.Y.
Cockayne, Michael, Community of the Celebration, Scotland
Cushing, Vincent, Washington Theological Coalition, Silver Spring, Md.
Dols, William, Immanuel on the Hill, Alexandria, Va.
Druhan, Ruth, Silver Spring, Md.
Fenhagen, James, The Hartford Seminary Foundation, Conn.
Houlihan, Rita Anne, Cenacle Retreat House, N.Y.

Hynes, Arlene, Arlington, Va.

Hunt, Dick, S.J. Ruah/The Isaac Hecker Spirituality Institute, Boston

Jones, Alan, Center for Christian Spirituality, General Theological Seminary, N.Y.

Keating, Thomas, St. Joseph's Abbey, Mass.

Kelsey, Morton, Notre Dame, Ind.

Kushner, Lawrence, Congregation Beth El, Ma.

McCarty, Shaun, S.T., Holy Trinity Mission Seminary, Silver Spring, Md.

Monroe, Terri, The Catholic Theological Union, Chicago

O'Connor, Elizabeth, Washington, D.C.

O'Hanlon, Daniel, Jesuit School of Theology, Berkeley

Payne, Richard, Paulist Press, NY

Prevallet, Elaine, S.L. Pendle Hill, Pa.

Raines, Robert, Kirkridge, Pa.

Reid, Thomas, Center for Human Development, University of Notre Dame, Ind.

Ripman, Hugh, Forthway Center for Advanced Studies, Washington, D.C.

Sasaki Roshi, Rev. Joshu, Cimarron Zen Center, Los Angeles and interpreter Gregory Campbell

Schachter, Zalman, Temple U., Pa.

Schneiders, Sandra, Jesuit School of Theology, Berkeley

Sommerfeldt, John, Center for Contemplative Studies, Western Michigan U.

Steere, Douglas, Haverford College, Pa.

Sullivan, Claire, Anchorhold, Potomac, Md.

Usinowicz, Stephen, Holy Cross Abbey, Berryville, Va.

Staff

The Rev. Henry Atkins, Community of the Advent, SHALEM, Washington, D.C.

Treadwell Atkins, Community of the Advent, SHALEM, Washington, D.C.

Cecilia Braveboy, Executive Director, Interreligious Association of Greater Washington, SHALEM, Washington, D.C.

Rev. Richard Byrne, St. Paul's College, SHALEM, Washington, D.C.

The Rev. Carole Crumley, Christ Episcopal Church, SHALEM, Washington, D.C.

The Rev. Tilden H. Edwards, Jr., Director of Shalem Institute for Spiritual Formation, Washington, D.C.

Joan Hickey, Adult Educator and Facilitator, SHALEM, Fairfax, Va.

Dolores Leckey, Executive Director, Secretariate of the Laity, National Conference Catholic Bishops, SHALEM, Arlington, Va.

Marlene Maier, Adult Educator; SHALEM, Silver Spring, Md.

Gerald May, M.D., Psychiatrist, SHALEM, Columbia, Md.

Judith McCallum Moe, Staff Assistant, SHALEM, Washington, D.C.

The Rev. William Moremen, First Congregational United Church of Christ, SHALEM, Washington, D.C.

The Rev. Roy Oswald, Director Metropolitan Ecumenical Training Center, SHALEM, Washington, D.C.

Dr. Parker Palmer, Dean of Studies, Pendle Hill, SHALEM, Wallingford, Pa.

Rabbi Daniel Polish, Associate Director of Synagogue Council of America, SHALEM, Rockville, Md.

Lynette Yount, Interreligious Association, Washington, D.C.